WOMEN'S EMANCIPATION DURING THE PROPHET'S LIFETIME

THE DEBATE ON PARTICIPATION IN SOCIAL LIFE AND ON FACE UNCOVERING

Volume 5

Abd al-Halim Abu Shuqqah

Translated and Edited by
Adil Salahi

KUBE
PUBLISHING

The Debate on participation in Social Life and on
Face Uncovering, Volume 5

First published in England by
Kube Publishing Ltd
Markfield Conference Centre,
Ratby Lane, Markfield,
Leicestershire, LE67 9SY,
United Kingdom
Tel: +44 (0) 1530 249230
Email: info@ kubepublishing.com
Website: www.kubepublishing.com

WOMEN'S EMANCIPATION DURING THE PROPHET'S LIFETIME

CIP data for this book is available from the British Library.

ISBN: 978-1-84774-189-9 *Paperback*
ISBN: 978-1-84774-190-5 *Ebook*

Translate and Edit by: Adil Salahi
Cover Design by: Nasir Cadir
Typeset by: nqaddoura@hotmail.com
Printed by: Imak Offset, Turkey

Contents

Transliteration Table

Consonants. Arabic

initial, unexpressed, medial and final: ء ʾ

ا	a	د	d	ض	ḍ	ك	k
ب	b	ذ	dh	ط	ṭ	ل	l
ت	t	ر	r	ظ	ẓ	م	m
ث	th	ز	z	ع	ʿ	ن	n
ج	j	س	s	غ	gh	هـ	h
ح	ḥ	ش	sh	ف	f	و	w
خ	kh	ص	ṣ	ق	q	ي	y

Vowels, diphthongs, etc.

short:	ـَـ	a	ـِـ	i	ـُـ	u
long:	ـَا	ā	ـُو	ū	ـِي	ī
diphthongs:			ـَوْ	aw		
			ـَيْ	ay		

CHAPTER I

Objections to Women's Participation in Social Life

THE DISCUSSION IN THIS CHAPTER WILL FOCUS ON THREE AREAS:

- One: Objections to the evidence on the permissibility of participation and meeting with men.
- Two: The evidence cited in support of prohibiting women's participation in social life and mixed meetings.
- Three: Responses to opponents' arguments.

One: Objections to the Evidence on the Permissibility of Participation and Meeting with Men

Objection 1

People claim that the texts speaking about the Prophet's actions apply to him alone; they cannot be given general application.

Several points should be raised in answer to this objection:

- It is natural that many texts should show aspects of the Prophet's life, because the Sunnah includes the Prophet's verbal statements, his actions and his approvals. Therefore, Muslims ever since the time of the Prophet's Companions have reported everything related to his sunnah because it incorporates legislation. The actions of the Prophet's Companions were only incidentally reported. This means that the Sunnah does not provide social or historical research into the different aspects of the life of the Prophet's Companions.

- Scholars of methodology and principles of jurisprudence make clear that special or individual application can only be confirmed on the basis of clear evidence. Such speciality cannot be confirmed on the basis of probability. Ibn Taymiyyah said: '... What God has made lawful to the Prophet remains lawful to all Muslims unless there is clear evidence that it is special to him.' Where do we find such evidence of special application in any of these texts?
- Scholars of Hadith and Fiqh, such as al-Bukhari and Ibn Ḥajar, commented on these hadiths and explained them, but they did not narrow their significance to make them of special application. On the contrary, they deduced from them confirmation that they are of general application. In the Foreword to Volume 2 of this series, we refer to several chapter headings in al-Bukhari's *Ṣaḥīḥ* confirming this, and we also cite in Chapter 5 of Volume 2 several quotes from Ibn Ḥajar with the same import.
- If, for argument's sake, we assume that some situations (nearly 50) apply to the Prophet in particular, because he is infallible, what about the women he used to meet? They are certainly not infallible. Also, what about the men who accompanied him in many situations (nearly 70)? What can be said about the nearly 150 situations that describe what the Prophet's Companions, not the Prophet, did?
- There are two factors to which we attach much importance in shaping up a consistent pattern of meetings during the Prophet's time. The first factor is that the Prophet represents the well balanced human state, or rather the state of human perfection and sound mental health. He never showed any leaning to either excess or lack of jealousy, either when men met his wives before or after they were screened, as God made permissible, or when he met other women. At the same time, he was the most perfectly pious of all people and absolutely keen to protect the honour of Muslims. He was perfectly

aware that it was his role to provide the best example to be followed by all believers. We will mention only two cases:

The first case was when the Prophet saw Asmā' bint Abu Bakr carrying a load that looked heavy, and she had a long way to go before she would arrive home. He offered to take her behind him on his mount, needless to say that this would have been without any physical contact. Asmā' recalled that her husband was a jealous man and she preferred to continue on her own. This is stated in a hadith related by al-Bukhari and Muslim. Would the Prophet make such an offer if it would hurt a reasonable husband? What prevented Asmā' from accepting the Prophet's offer was that her husband, al-Zubayr, was especially jealous.

The other case is the Prophet's attitude when he saw in a dream that he was in heaven and he saw a woman performing *wudu*, i.e. ablution, close to a palace. When he was told that the palace belonged to 'Umar ibn al-Khaṭṭāb, he remembered 'Umar's jealousy and turned away without looking inside. This is also mentioned in a hadith related by al-Bukhari and Muslim.

The Prophet did not turn away from the palace because he felt that his presence was not appropriate, he was rather considerate of 'Umar's feelings as he knew him to be very jealous. 'Umar disliked his wife going to the mosque to take part in congregational prayer, but he did not allow his jealousy to go as far as acting against the Prophet's instructions: 'Do not stop women servants of God from attending God's mosques.' (Related by al-Bukhari)

Such was the Prophet's guidance. Yet he said: 'Do you wonder at Sa'd's jealousy? I am more jealous than him, and God is more jealous than me.' (Related by al-Bukhari and Muslim) He also said: 'No one is more jealous than God. It is because of this that He has forbidden shameful deeds.' (Related by al-Bukhari)

God's Messenger is more jealous than Sa'd and more than all people, but it is sound jealousy that steers away from what is shameful and from compromising situations. Should we not organize our society according to the Prophet's guidance? Or do we prefer to organize it according to people's prejudices, even though they may be the best of people?

The other factor is that the Prophet considered the woman as an honourable human being, who is man's partner in this life, and not a mere sex object. Life requires this human being to exercise various activities in the same way as it requires man to exercise certain activities, with clear distinction between the two. Yet even this distinction varies as women, societies and generations vary. There is considerable difference between a married woman and an unmarried one, a mother and a childless woman. Likewise, there is great difference between rural and urban societies, and between our generation and that of our grandparents.

☙ Perhaps the life of the Prophet's Companions does not give us a clear picture of meetings with women in the same way as we have in respect of the Prophet's own life and meetings. This is due in a large measure to the fact that believers were keen to monitor and report the Prophet's sunnah, and did not do the same in respect of his Companions. It may also be due in some cases to some personal considerations that are not related to Islamic law. Moreover, the example we should follow is provided by God's Messenger, and the Sunnah is his own actions, not the actions of anyone else. His Companions followed his example as they could, in their own respective circumstances. Yet, they collaborated in the preservation of his sunnah, monitoring all his actions, and transmitted these to the following Muslim generations so that they would serve as an explanation of the Qur'an and its teachings. Nevertheless, the texts we have about the life of the Prophet's Companions give us a very clear picture when we understand these in the light of the Prophet's sunnah.

Objection 2

People say that the incidents of the Prophet's Companions' meetings with women are individual cases, with no general significance or application.

In response to this objection we say:

- These cases are too numerous and varied to be considered individual cases with no general significance. When we count them, relying only on the texts of the hadith in the two *Ṣaḥīḥ* anthologies of al-Bukhari and Muslim, we find that there were nearly 70 cases when the Prophet's Companions were with the Prophet as they met women, and there were nearly 150 cases when they met women on their own, without the Prophet being present.
- Scholars of methodology and principles of Islamic law state that whatever is confirmed to apply to one person during the lifetime of the Prophet (peace be upon him) also applies to everyone else, unless there is clear evidence restricting its application to that person. The objectors do not provide any indication that may serve as evidence for such restriction.
- Leading Hadith scholars, such as al-Bukhari and Ibn Ḥajar, do not consider these cases as individual incidents applicable to particular people. This is clear in al-Bukhari's chapter headings and Ibn Ḥajar's comments which we quoted earlier.

Objection 3

People say that the incidents of meetings between men and women reported in the hadiths were for legitimate necessities. A necessity relaxes prohibition.

In answer we have the following points:

- If meeting between men and women is forbidden, what evidence is there to show that it is forbidden?
- May we request the objectors to reflect on the texts which speak of the cases of women's participation in social life and their meetings with men. Let them, then, tell us which of these were for a clear necessity. We are here speaking of a necessity that relaxes what is forbidden and makes it lawful.
- If all these cases of meetings were for pressing necessities, how come that highly distinguished scholars of Hadith and Fiqh, such as al-Bukhari and Ibn Ḥajar, overlooked this? How come they deduced from them rulings that allow many cases of meetings, as we have learnt from al-Bukhari's chapter headings and Ibn Ḥajar's commentary?

Objection 4

People say that society during the Prophet's lifetime was virtuous where temptation was at a minimum. This is the opposite of our societies today where immorality is common and temptation is very strong.

Our answer is as follows:

- There is no doubt that the society of the Prophet's Companions was better than all others, as the Prophet describes their generation as the best. Yet every society includes people of varying degrees of strength and weakness. During the

Prophet's lifetime, there were different types of people in Madinah. Some were of the class of Abu Bakr and 'Umar, while others were weak such as those whose hearts needed to be won over to Islam. Others were Bedouins who embraced Islam but were not firm believers. There were among them some youths with little experience, and others who were absolute hypocrites and others still who betrayed some aspect of hypocrisy. All these types used to come to the mosque and attend the hajj season.

- We are talking about a meeting that is serious, observing the rules of propriety and decorum that God has legislated. We are addressing Muslims who are keen to follow the guidance provided by God's Messenger (peace be upon him) and who offer their five obligatory prayers every day. They may include those who are weak alongside those who are strong in faith. As for transgressors who observe no rules of propriety or decency, they go ahead with their indecency, caring nothing for whatever we say.
- If we are to narrow the areas of contact and meeting because of the spread of loose morality in society, such restriction should be within the limits that protect Muslim men and women from such lack of morality. We cannot issue a ruling of strict prohibition applicable to all areas.
- The claim of the need to preserve society against temptation and prevent the causes of immoral behaviour is a very serious one. Therefore, we shall discuss it in detail in Volume 6 of this series.

Two: The evidence cited in support of prohibiting women's participation in social life and mixed meetings

Evidence 1

> The Qur'anic verse that says: 'And stay quietly in your homes.' (33: 33)

In answer we may say the following:

- This verse and the ones before it and those that follow it are addressed to the Prophet's wives. Ibn Ḥajar said: 'This verse states a clear order given to the Prophet's wives. Therefore, Umm Salamah used to say: "No camel shall carry me until I meet the Prophet (peace be upon him)."'
- One thing that confirms this order applies only to the Prophet's wives is that 'Umar ibn al-Khaṭṭāb did not permit

them to perform the hajj except when he performed his own last pilgrimage. Ibn Ḥajar said: 'The Prophet said to 'Ā'ishah when she asked him whether women could go on military expeditions for jihad: "For you [i.e. women], the best and most fitting jihad is the hajj." She and others understood this to mean encouragement to do the hajj several times. The Prophet's statement is also understood to limit the meaning of his other saying to his wives: "This time, then staying at home." As for the verse that says: 'Stay quietly in your homes,' it appears that 'Umar was uncertain as to what it entailed, then he recognized the clear meaning of the evidence 'Ā'ishah cited. Therefore, he permitted the Prophet's wives to go on hajj towards the end of his reign.'

- Let us, for argument's sake, assume that the verse is addressed to all Muslim women. The Sunnah provides the explanation of the Qur'an. We have quoted plenty of hadith texts that speak of women's participation in social life and their meetings with men. These provide a clear picture of how women believers implemented the order of 'staying quietly at home' during the Prophet's lifetime, showing that this order did not prevent them from participation in social life. This means that by word, action and approval, the Prophet permitted women's participation in social life and their meeting with men. All this explains the meaning of what the Qur'an says.

Evidence 2

> The Qur'an says: 'When you ask them for something, do so from behind a screen: this makes for greater purity for your hearts and theirs.' (33: 53)

We have several points to make in answer:

- The word *ḥijāb* mentioned in this verse means a screen behind which a woman stays. Thus, the verse means that the

Prophet's wives had to stay behind a screen when unrelated men spoke to them. Thus, they spoke to them without seeing them. In this work, we use the term *ḥijāb* in this sense, which is used in the Qur'an and the hadiths. We do not use it in the common sense of women wearing long and wide clothing to cover their bodies. There is much difference between the two and the Islamic rulings concerning them. The first and correct meaning, i.e. the screen, applied to the Prophet's wives in particular. The second and commonly used meaning is obligatory to all Muslim women. We must not confuse the two meanings or rulings.

- The same verse makes clear that its address is meant for the Prophet's wives in particular. The verse concludes with certain instructions which we take to be one of the reasons for imposing the screening on the Prophet's wives. God says: 'Moreover, it does not behove you to give offence to God's Messenger, just as it would not behove you ever to marry his widows after he has passed away. That is certainly an enormity in God's sight.' (33: 53) Chapter 2 in this volume is devoted to the explanation of the *ḥijāb* being applicable to the Prophet's wives only and that they could not, and should not, be emulated by other women in this respect.

What was specifically applicable to the Prophet's wives only was to always remain behind a screen when speaking to men. Occasional screening of Muslim women generally is acceptable, in the same way as their occasional meeting with men is also permissible.

- The texts of the hadiths we quoted explain how Muslim men and women met during the Prophet's lifetime, in all areas of life, without *ḥijāb*, i.e. without a screen separating men from women. Had screening been a common practice, or had it been recommended to emulate the Prophet's wives with regard to the *ḥijāb*, the Prophet's noble Companions, men and women, would have been the first to implement it. In other words, had it been for the general good, they would have done it. No one can claim that this was a sunnah but they did not know it, or that they knew it and ignored it. Far be it from them to do so.

We will now refer to an important point that is closely related to the verse that mentions the *ḥijāb*. If, for argument's sake, we accept that it is recommended for women to emulate the Prophet's wives regarding the *ḥijāb* – which is something that is not acceptable – we have the following observations to make:

- The *ḥijāb* may be recommended when it is associated with making things easier for believers, men and women. This can only be the case when it is used on some occasions and in certain circumstances, but not in all situations. If it becomes the standard practice for dealings between men and women, it will only lead to restriction and will make things especially difficult. Yet God says: 'He has laid no hardship on you in anything that pertains to religion.' (22: 78) It is authentically reported that the Prophet said: 'Whenever God's Messenger (peace be upon him) was given a choice between two alternatives, he always chose the easier, unless it was sinful.' (Related by al-Bukhari and Muslim)
- If the *ḥijāb* and the concept of 'purity of hearts' which is associated with it are clear virtues and recommended to us, we need to consider all such virtues and recommendations, seeking to do what is more important in every situation. To only look at one virtue, which is 'heart purity' and shut our eyes to others, or to ignore the more important of such virtues, such as the pursuit of knowledge, advocacy of what is good and doing what is beneficial, is not acceptable to Islam which stresses the importance of prioritization in both what is obligatory and what is recommended.

- It is important that as we seek to do what is 'purer for hearts', which is recommended, we do not neglect some other duties. The pursuit of knowledge, advocacy of what is good and doing what is beneficial are virtues that may become duties at times.
- To sum up: seeking what promotes 'purity of hearts' may become a slippery way with two branches. The first is to do one virtue while neglecting one or others that are more important, and the second is to do a recommended virtue while neglecting one or several duties. This means that when we seek the maximum degree of heart purity for women, we are happy to leave them with a minimum share of education and knowledge, depriving them of many types of good action, such as maintaining ties of good neighbourliness and ties of kinship, extending good action towards them, urging the doing of what is good and refraining from what is wrong and evil. Ibn Ḥajar states the truth as he says: '... It is permissible to prevent doing some desirable matters if it is feared that doing them will lead to the neglect of rights that are either obligatory or recommended in a higher degree than those desirable matters.'

☙ Another point is important to bear in mind. The *ḥijab* leads to greater purity of hearts, and it is also more comfortable for people. It relieves them of the trouble of resisting temptation, the need to lower one's gaze and resist Satan's promptings. We may repeat here our earlier argument that choosing what is more comfortable is permissible unless it is contrary to a certain duty or leads to missing out on an ascertained or more important benefit. We mentioned duties and benefits in Volume 2, which is devoted to women's participation in social life. What is important is to warn against doing what is more comfortable rather than leaving all fields of life open for women to grow intellectually and socially. This is, indeed, the way for the advancement of society and making life easier for Muslim men and women. Moreover, it checks rebellion against Islamic rules which is caused by strictness and rigidity. We remind everyone that life is not only adherence to the right faith, but also involves a life-long struggle.

- It is also important to recognize the role of familiarity and habit in social relations. Familiarity reduces sensitivity when meeting people of the opposite sex. This makes things easier for both parties. A woman who is not used to meeting men will certainly feel greatly sensitive and embarrassed when there is a need for her to meet men. Her husband, father or brother will also feel the embarrassment. It may happen that all of them would prefer to forgo that need and what it could bring of goodness to them, regardless of how important that is to the woman or to society, rather than go through such an embarrassing situation. The same applies to men. The one who is familiar with meeting women from time to time, as the need arises, will not feel the embarrassment a man who is unfamiliar with meeting women will feel when he needs to meet them.
- Finally, we ask our brothers, the objectors: Did God's Messenger (peace be upon him) disregard the 'purity of hearts' of Muslim men and women when he allowed them to meet in all the forms and ways we mentioned, without there being a screen between them? Far be it from him to entertain any such disregard. Or, was he looking at 'purity of hearts' together with making things easier on the one hand and looking at people's needs and interests on the other? Had that degree of 'purity' referred to in the above-quoted verse been recommended for all Muslims in all situations, God's Messenger would have taken some arrangements to ensure its observation. He would have, for example, arranged for a screen to separate the rows of men and women in the mosque. He would have allocated different times for the *ṭawāf* of men and women, and

he would have taken women away from where he used to sit with his Companions to listen to the women's problems and questions and to give them rulings pertaining to them. He would have taken such measures so that men would not see women and women would not see men!

Evidence 3

> This is the hadith quoting the Prophet: 'Beware of entry to women's places.' A man from the Anṣār said: 'Messenger of God, how about an in-law relative?' He said: 'An in-law is death.'

In answer, we say that the prohibition here applies to being alone with a woman, not any entry of women's places when others are present. This is confirmed by the following:

Such is the understanding of the leading Hadith scholars, such as al-Bukhari and al-Tirmidhī, and the understanding of the leading commentators on hadith, such as Ibn Ḥajar in his commentary on al-Bukhari's *Ṣaḥīḥ* and al-Nawawī in his commentary on Muslim's *Ṣaḥīḥ*. The same is the understanding of highly distinguished Fiqh scholars such as Ibn Daqīq al-ʿĪd and Ibn Taymiyyah.

Al-Bukhari enters this hadith in a chapter to which he gives the following heading: 'No man may be alone with a woman except a *maḥram*, and visiting a woman when her husband is absent.' He then lists this hadith, 'Beware of entry to women's places' and follows it with the hadith: 'No man may be alone with a woman unless accompanied by a *maḥram*.'

In his book *Fatḥ al-Bārī*, Ibn Ḥajar says: 'The Prophet said that "an in-law is death". It is said this means that being alone with an in-law may lead to the ruin of one's faith if they commit a sin, or to real death if an act of adultery is committed and punished by stoning, or to the ruin of the woman if her husband feels so upset that he divorces her. All this has been mentioned by al-Qurṭubī, while al-Ṭabarī said that it means that "for a man to be alone with his brother's wife or his nephew's wife is considered like death. The Arabs often use the word 'death' to describe what they find repugnant."'

In his commentary on Muslim's *Ṣaḥīḥ*, al-Nawawī said: 'The Prophet said that "an in-law is death". This means that this is something to be feared as more evil than other situations. It causes stronger temptation. An in-law can more easily find his way to a woman and be alone with her. In this context, an 'in-law' refers to the husband's relatives other than his parents and sons. The latter, i.e. parents and sons are *maḥrams*, i.e. unmarriageable relatives, to his wife and any of them may be alone with her and they cannot be described as 'death'. The Prophet is referring to the husband's brother, nephew, uncle, cousin, etc. These are non-*maḥrams* and people take an easy attitude in their cases. Therefore, for a man to be alone with his brother's wife means death... *Qadi* 'Iyāḍ said: "It means that being alone with an in-law may lead to temptation and ruining one's faith. Hence the Prophet compares it to death."'

Al-Tirmidhī relates the hadith in his *Sunan* and says: 'This hadith narrated by 'Uqbah ibn 'Āmir is good and authentic. The censure of entry to women's places is understood on the same lines as another hadith quoting the Prophet (peace be upon him): "Whenever a man is alone with a woman, Satan is the third." The meaning of an "in-law" is her husband's brother, suggesting that the Prophet disapproved of him being alone with her.'

Ibn Daqīq al-'Īd said: 'The hadith is evidence confirming the prohibition of being alone with an unrelated person of the opposite sex. The Prophet's warning: "Beware of entry to women's places" applies specifically to non-*maḥrams* and generally to others. Another point must be considered. This is, that entry means being alone with her. If this is not the case, no prohibition applies.'

Ibn Taymiyyah was asked 'whether it is permissible for a man to visit his brother's wife, or his paternal or maternal cousin?' He answered: 'It is forbidden for him to be alone with her. If he visits her along with others, so that he is not alone with her and there is no suspicion, it is permissible.'

Further, we may say that it is necessary to understand within this context of being alone with a woman that we can reconcile this hadith with many others that permit entry to women's places without one man being alone with one woman. These hadiths include:

i. The verbal sunnah that sets the norms when men visit women:

- Ibn 'Abbās narrated: God's Messenger (peace be upon him) said: 'A woman may not travel unless accompanied by a man who is *maḥram*. No man may enter her place unless a *maḥram* is present with her.' (Related by al-Bukhari)
- 'Abdullāh ibn 'Amr ibn al-'Āṣ narrated: '... Then God's Messenger (peace be upon him) stood on the platform and said: "After this day of mine, no man may enter the place of a woman whose husband is absent unless he is accompanied by one or two men."' (Related by Muslim)

ii. The practical sunnah clarifies some reasons for visiting women:

TAKING CARE

- Anas ibn Mālik narrated: 'When the Prophet (peace be upon him) passed near Umm Sulaym's place, he would drop in and greet her.' (Related by al-Bukhari) In another version: 'The Prophet (peace be upon him) visited us when there was only myself, my mother and my maternal aunt Umm Ḥarām. He said: "Stand up and I shall lead you in prayer."' (Related by Muslim)
- Anas narrated: 'The Prophet (peace be upon him) visited Umm Sulaym and she served him dates and ghee...' (Related by al-Bukhari)

Ibn Ḥajar said: 'This hadith highlights several points... that it is permissible to enter someone's home when he is not in. The various narrations of this case do not mention that Abu Ṭalḥah [Umm Sulaym's husband] was present.'

Visiting an ill person

- 'Ā'ishah said: 'God's Messenger (peace be upon him) visited Ḍubā'ah bint al-Zubayr. He said to her: "Do you want to perform the hajj?" She said: "By God, I am often ill." He said: "Then go for hajj and make a condition. You say: 'My Lord, my place of release [from consecration] is wherever You detain me.'" She was married to al-Miqdād ibn al-Aswad.' (Related by al-Bukhari and Muslim)

Offering condolences

- Umm al-'Alā' narrated: '... God's Messenger (peace be upon him) entered. I said: "May God bestow mercy on you, Abu al-Sā'ib..."' (Related by al-Bukhari)

Offering congratulations

- Al-Rubayyi' bint Mu'awwidh said: 'The Prophet visited me the morning after my wedding and he sat on my bed as you are seated now. We had maids playing on the tambourine...' (Related by al-Bukhari)

Attending to what is needed

- 'Ā'ishah said: '... [God's Messenger] said: "By God, I have known nothing of my wife except what is good, and they mention a man of whom I have known nothing but good. He only entered my home in my company..."' (Related by al-Bukhari and Muslim)

iii. The Prophet's companions' practice: Different purposes motivated the Prophet's companions to visit women and enter their places.

Seeking knowledge

Asmā' bint 'Umays narrated: '... Abu Mūsā and those who travelled by boat came to me in groups asking me about this hadith.' (Related by al-Bukhari and Muslim)

Paying a visit

Abu Juḥayfah narrated: 'The Prophet (peace be upon him) established a bond of brotherhood between Salmān and Abu al-Dardā'.[1] Salmān visited Abu al-Dardā' and he found Umm al-Dardā' wearing simple clothes. He asked her the reason...' (Related by al-Bukhari)

Enquiring after people

Qays ibn Abi Ḥāzim narrated: 'Abu Bakr visited a woman from the tribe of Aḥmus called Zaynab bint al-Muhājir...' (Related by al-Bukhari)

Evidence 4

The following hadith was narrated by Anas: 'Apart from his wives' homes, the Prophet (peace be upon him) did not enter any home in Madinah except Umm Sulaym's. He was asked about it and he said: 'It is compassion to her: her brother was killed [fighting] with me.' (Related by al Bukhari and Muslim)

1. The bond of brotherhood was meant to establish closer relations between the Prophet's companions. The Prophet established it between totally unrelated Muslims. Salman was of Persian origin while Abu al-Dardā' belonged to the Khazraj tribe of the Anṣār.

In answer we say that we need to understand this hadith in the light of the many hadiths that speak about cases of participation in social life and meetings. These state that the Prophet entered many homes in Madinah. His visits to Umm Sulaym were many and frequent, attracting the attention of his Companions. Hence, they asked him the reason and he gave them the explanation.

Al-Bukhari enters this hadith in a chapter with the heading: 'The merit of one who equips a fighter or succeeds him doing well.' The following comments are stated in *Fatḥ al-Bārī*: 'The hadith mentions that "the Prophet did not enter any home in Madinah except Umm Sulaym's." Al-Ḥumaydī said: "Perhaps he meant frequently..." Ibn al-Tīn said: "He visited Umm Sulaym often..." Ibn al-Munayyir said: "Anas's hadith is consistent with the chapter heading as it says, 'or succeeds him doing well', because this is more general than specifying whether it was during the fighter's lifetime or after his death. The Prophet used to console Umm Sulaym by visiting her, explaining his action on the basis that her brother was killed fighting with him. Thus, he succeeded her brother by taking care of his family. This is an aspect of the Prophet's maintaining good relations."'

To sum up what is negated in this hadith by Anas is a particular aspect of visiting, not visits altogether.

Evidence 5

> The hadith narrated by Umm Salamah: 'I was at God's Messenger's (peace be upon him) and Maymūnah was with him when Ibn Umm Maktūm came over. This was after we were commanded to be screened. The Prophet said to us: "Go behind a screen." We said: "Messenger of God, is he not blind and cannot see or recognize us?" The Prophet said: "Are you two also blind? Do you not see him?"'

The following points may be given in answer:

- The two women mentioned in this hadith were wives of the Prophet, and the Qur'anic verse that orders their screening says: 'When you ask the Prophet's wives for something, do so from behind a screen: this makes for greater purity for your hearts and theirs.' (33: 53) This means that if men did not see the Prophet's wives they gained greater purity of their hearts, and similarly that greater purity for the hearts of the Prophet's wives was gained by not seeing men. Hence, the Prophet said to them what he said. In short, the point here is that the screening applied only to the Prophet's wives, so that they did not meet men in the same place without a screen between them.
- The Prophet told his two wives not to look at Ibn Umm Maktūm because they were ordered to remain behind a screen. Yet he said to Fātimah bint Qays: 'Observe your waiting period in the home of your cousin Ibn Umm Maktūm, as he is a blind man.' This meant that she would stay throughout her waiting period in his home, under the same roof. This meant that she would mix with him in his home for the entire waiting period, not a matter of an hour or so. She would definitely be seeing him, and there was no harm in this. All this confirms that the order in Umm Salamah's hadith applies to the Prophet's wives. This is clearly indicated by her clarification: 'after we were commanded to be screened.'
- That the Prophet's rhetorical question, 'Are you two also blind?' applied only to the Prophet's wives is further confirmed by Imam Ahmad. Al-Athram said: 'I said to Abu 'Abdullāh [i.e. Imam Ahmad]: "It appears that Nabhān's [who narrated from Umm Salamah] hadith refers to the Prophet's wives in particular and the hadith concerning Fāṭimah bint Qays applies to all people?" He said: "Yes."' Abu Dāwūd also states this, commenting after having entered the hadith:

'This applied to the Prophet's wives in particular. Do you not note that Fāṭimah bint Qays spent her waiting period at Ibn Umm Maktūm's? The Prophet said to her: "Observe your waiting period in the home of your cousin Ibn Umm Maktūm, as he is a blind man, and you can put off your [outer] garments at his place."'

Evidence 6

The following hadith is narrated by Umm Ḥumayd, the wife of Abi Ḥumayd al-Sāʿidī. She said that she went to the Prophet and said: 'Messenger of God, I love praying with you.' He said: 'I know that. Yet, your prayer in your bedroom is better than your prayer in your front room; and your prayer in your front room is better than your prayer in your yard; and prayer in your yard is better than prayer in your people's mosque; and prayer in your people's mosque is better than prayer in the main mosque.'

We have several points to make in answer:

- This hadith says to Umm Ḥumayd: 'Your prayer in your bedroom is better than your prayer in your front room and your prayer in your front room is better than your prayer in your yard.' Normally, in the front room and the yard there would be women and also men who are close relatives. The presence of men who are unrelated to the woman is rare. If it is claimed that the rare presence of such unrelated men is the reason for the preference given to the bedroom over the front room and to the front room over the yard, we say this means that their presence at other times, when the woman is not praying, is fine. In other words, it is seeing her when she is praying that is the problem. Does this mean that what is encouraged here is to hide the prayer and keep it away from men's eyes, rather than hiding the woman's body?

- Does this statement of graded preference aim to keep women away from meeting men, even though in a situation of modesty and propriety? Had it been so, women would not have been recommended to stay in the mosque for *i'tikāf*, or to take part in occasional prayers such as funeral and eclipse prayers. Nor would they have been encouraged to attend study circles. Indeed, it would have been more preferable for a woman not to visit the place of *i'tikaf* in the mosque and she would not have been encouraged to meet other women in the mosque, or volunteer to clean the mosque and remove any litter from it. We would not have had the insistent order that women should attend the Eid Prayer and the order would not have specified that young women who normally stay at home and even women having their period should attend this prayer. Indeed, women would not have been encouraged to perform voluntary hajj after they had performed their obligatory hajj, because the hajj involves not merely meeting men, but also pushing their way through places that are crowded with men and women.
- Had it been preferable that women offer all their prayers at home, the noble female companions of the Prophet would also have been the first to observe and maintain this preference. The Prophet would have drawn the attention of those women who brought their young children to the mosque to this. Yet, instead, if a young child cried during the prayer and the Prophet heard the child crying, he would shorten his prayer. Would the Prophet accept the prayer being cut short, allowing the congregation to miss out on a longer prayer for the sake of a less preferable matter, which was a woman's attending the congregational prayer? Would he not have told the women to do the preferable option of praying at home so that they would allow the men to have their longer prayer, which could also have been considered preferable? The Prophet would also have drawn the attention of the women who were keen to attend the 'Ishā' congregational prayer in the mosque to the preferability of delaying 'Ishā'. What happened, in fact,

was that the Prophet once took a long time before coming out to lead the 'Ishā' Prayer and people started to doze off as they waited for him. Then 'Umar shouted aloud: 'Women and children are dozing off.' Yet the Prophet explained that this delay was preferable. The question then is: Why did the Prophet immediately come out for the prayer on hearing what 'Umar said, when he had already stressed that the delay is preferable? Why would he sacrifice what is preferable for the sake of the less preferable, which is women coming to the mosque?

- Had it always been better for women to offer their prayers at home, 'Umar ibn al-Khaṭṭāb's wife would have not insisted on attending the congregational prayer in the mosque, when she was reminded that her husband disliked her going out at night. It would have encouraged her to respect his feelings in this matter. She would then have done the better option for herself and earned the reward for pleasing her husband. Ibn 'Umar would have reminded her of such preferability when he encouraged her to respect his father's feelings. Furthermore, had it always been better for women to pray at home, 'Abdullāh ibn 'Umar would not have encouraged people not to prevent their women from going to the mosque. His son said that he would prevent them, but he did not cite this preferability as an argument against his father.
- The scenarios of men and women meeting and participating in events in the mosque during the Prophet's lifetime are greatly significant in many ways, including:

  i. That the Prophet approved that women offered their prayers with him in his mosque from the first day of his arrival in Madinah to the end of his blessed life.
  ii. The consistency of women attending congregational prayers in their local mosques outside Madinah. This means that their attendance was not limited to the Prophet's mosque only.
  iii. The Prophet's clear order to men that they must not deny women their share of attending mosques.

iv. The distinguished ones among the Prophet's female companions used to attend the congregational prayer in the mosque. These included Asmā' bint Abu Bakr, Umm al-Faḍl, Fāṭima bint Qays, ʿAbdullāh ibn Masʿūd's wife Zaynab, Umm al-Dardā', ʿUmar ibn al-Khaṭṭāb's wife ʿĀtikah bint Zayd and al-Rubayyiʿ bint Muʿawwidh.
v. A large number of women used to attend the congregational prayer in the Prophet's mosque, with the women making up more than one full row.
vi. Women went to the mosque for a variety of reasons, including attending the prayers that included reciting the Qur'an aloud which are Fajr, Maghrib and ʿIshā', taking part in Friday Prayer, voluntary night prayer, eclipse prayer, *iʿtikāf*, visiting someone who is in *iʿtikāf*, attending a public meeting with the ruler, watching the play of the Abyssinian visitors, cleaning the mosque and spending time with other women, etc. (Reference may be made to Chapter 4, Volume 2 of this abridged version.)

We believe that, taken together, these points confirm that praying at home is better for a woman if her taking the trouble to attend the congregational prayer in the mosque leads to the negligence of some needs of her home and family. In other words, it is preferable that a woman prays at home when she needs to attend to her home and family at the time of congregational prayer in the mosque. This is often the general situation of most women. Therefore, we say it is preferable for a woman to pray at home if going to the mosque to join congregational prayer causes her some difficulty or inconvenience.

Imam al-Sarakhsī said: 'The duty of going to attend the Friday Prayer does not apply to a traveller, woman and a person who is sick. This exemption is not related to the prayer itself but to the difficulty and inconvenience involved. If such people undertake the trouble to attend, they fulfil the duty as the rest of people.' We say the same concerning women and congregational prayer: they are exempted from the sunnah of going to the mosque to join congregational prayer. This is not due to the prayer itself but rather to the difficulty and inconvenience involved. If a woman undertakes the trouble to attend, she fulfils the sunnah as do the rest of the congregation.

This specific understanding of the preference of praying at home for women is similar to giving higher importance to the woman taking care of her children and family home than joining a jihad campaign. This applies when taking such care of home and family is needed, which is the general situation of most women. If the need is no longer there, and a woman has no such duties, or she is relieved of such duties, she may join a jihad campaign as a volunteer, hoping to be a martyr and eager to earn God's reward. The following hadith, which al-Bukhari enters under the chapter heading: 'Supplication for joining jihad and martyrdom for men and women': Anas ibn Mālik reports: "The Prophet used to visit Umm Ḥarām bint Milḥān... He once slept [at her place] and when he woke up, he smiled. She asked him what caused him to smile. He said: 'I was shown a group of my followers going for jihad, riding into the sea, looking like kings on their thrones...' She said: 'Messenger of God! Pray to God to make me one of them.' He prayed for her as she requested... She went on the maritime expedition during the reign of Muʿāwiyah ibn Abi Sufyān, and when she disembarked, she fell off her mount and died." (Related by al-Bukhari and Muslim)

A woman often finds herself unable to attend congregational prayer in order to listen to the Qur'an recited by an imam who is a good reciter and chooses long passages, or to listen to a talk after the prayer, or to the address in Friday Prayer, or to meet other Muslim women and cooperate with them in some good action, due to her family duties, including pregnancy and child care. Yet, if she undertakes the trouble to go to the mosque for any such purpose, she earns the reward of the good purpose for which she goes. God's Messenger says the truth: 'Whoever comes to the mosque for a purpose, that is what he gets.' (Related by Abu Dāwūd) This meaning is highlighted by a quote attributed to Imam Mālik: 'Whoever attends the Friday Prayer, other than men, hoping for the benefit it gives, is recommended to take a bath before it and observe all other recommended manners.'

The Prophet said: 'The best prayer is when a person prays at home, except the obligatory prayers.' (Related by al-Bukhari and Muslim) Nevertheless, the Prophet permitted his companions to join him in praying the voluntary night prayers during Ramadan for several nights, so that they could listen to his recitation of the Qur'an in long prayers. Not all of them had memorized long parts of the Qur'an. He did not wish to continue this practice because he feared that it would become obligatory for them. When he passed away, there was no longer such fear. It was then that the Prophet's companions, men and women, gathered in the mosque to offer this voluntary night prayer during Ramadan. This became a standard practice by Muslims everywhere. To emphasize the importance of listening to the Qur'an being recited in prayer by an imam who is a good reciter and memorizer, the Prophet approved that a young boy leading his people in prayer because he was the one who had memorized more of the Qur'an than anyone else among them. 'Amr ibn Salamah narrated from his father; he said: 'By God, I am coming back after having met the Prophet indeed. He said: ... "Let the one who had learnt most of the Qur'an lead you in prayer." They checked and I was the one who had learnt most of the Qur'an, because I used to learn from travellers. They put me forward to lead the prayer. I was only six or seven years of age.' (Related by al-Bukhari)

In his *Sunan* anthology, Abu Dāwūd relates the following hadith with a sound chain of transmission: 'Umm Waraqah bint 'Abdullāh ibn al-Ḥārith had learnt the Qur'an. She sought the Prophet's permission to have someone call the *adhān* at her home and he granted her permission... He ordered her to lead the people in her household in prayer.' In his book *Subul al-Salām*, al-Ṣan'ānī says: 'The hadith provides evidence that it is appropriate for a woman to lead the members of her household in prayer, even if they include a man. She had a man who called the *adhān*... It appears that he and her slave and maid were the people she led in prayer. Abu Thawr, al-Muzanī and al-Ṭabarī are of the view that this is valid, but the great majority of scholars disapprove.'

Scholars emphasize the merit of listening to the Qur'an being recited in prayer, to the extent that Imam Ahmad and some Ḥanbalī scholars express a view which is contrary to the ruling of most scholars. Ibn Taymiyyah said: 'That a woman who has memorized the Qur'an leads unlettered men in the night prayer during Ramadan is permissible according to the well-known view of Ahmad.'

In his book *al-Mughnī*, Ibn Qudāmah says: 'It is not permissible for a woman to be the imam when a man is present, whether in obligatory or voluntary prayer according to the view of scholars generally... Some of our scholars said that she may lead men in the Tarāwīḥ Prayer during Ramadan, but she stands behind them.'

We think that the mention by these scholars of the Tarāwīḥ Prayer in particular implies that the concession for a woman to lead the prayer applies only when she has memorized the Qur'an better than the men in the congregation. It is well-known that it is recommended to prolong the Qur'anic recitation in Tarāwīḥ Prayer.

- Ibn Daqīq al-'Īd comments on the hadith quoting the Prophet: 'A person's prayer with a congregation earns a reward twenty-five times higher than his prayer at home or at his place in the market.' He refers to women going to the mosque for congregational prayer and says: 'Wherever it is recommended for a woman to go to the mosque, she will earn the same reward as a man, because in respect of rewarding people's actions, being masculine or feminine is not considered.'

On the point of the preferability of women praying at home, Ibn Ḥazm has the following to say, which deserves careful consideration:

> As we consider the matter, we realize that the women's coming to the mosque or the prayer place is an extra action, added to the prayer. It involves effort at dawn, in the dark, in crowded places, in hot weather at midday, in the rain and cold, etc. If the merit of such action is abrogated, then there are only two possibilities: either the woman's prayer in the mosque or the prayer place is equal to her prayer at home, and then all this action becomes meaningless and pointless. It cannot be viewed otherwise... The other alternative is what the objectors say, namely that women's prayer in the mosque or the prayer place is lesser in merit than praying at home. In this case such undertaking becomes necessarily sinful, reducing the merit of the prayer. No added action reduces the merit of any particular prayer unless that action is a forbidden one. It is not possible otherwise. This is not to be treated as omitting some desirable action in prayer. A desirable action increases the reward of the prayer when done. However, its omission does not involve a sinful action; it is simply an omission of a good action. A person who deliberately does something in his prayer, resulting in depriving him of a portion of the reward of that prayer if completed without that action, actually does something forbidden. There is no doubt about that. When something is discouraged, i.e. *makrūh*, it is not sinful and does not detract from an action; it only means that it earns no reward and incurs no punishment. Sin and spoiling action are the result

of only what is forbidden. All people on earth agree that God's Messenger (peace be upon him) never stopped women from offering their prayers with him in his mosque and this remained true to the end of his life. Nor did the Rightly-Guided Caliphs who succeeded him stop women coming to the mosque for prayer. This means that their presence was not abrogated. As such, it is a meritorious action. Had it not been so, the Prophet would not have approved of it, and would not have let them take this trouble if it was of no benefit to them, or rather if it would harm them.

- We say finally that this hadith narrated by Umm Ḥumayd, and other hadiths encouraging women to stay away from men's society, need further and more careful investigation to ascertain the authenticity of their chains of transmission. They contradict the Prophet's guidance, reflected in the practical implementation by Muslim women during the Prophet's lifetime. Such implementation is mentioned in numerous hadiths, running into hundreds. As such, these hadiths are definitely authentic and give clear meaning. As such, they may attain together to the degree of *mutawātir*. We mentioned many of these in Chapter 4 of Volume 2 of this abridged version. Even if the hadiths giving the contrary meaning prove to have authentic chains of transmission, they must be understood in a way that reconciles them with those *mutawātir* hadiths which have more authentic chains of transmission and are clearer in import.

Evidence 7

The hadith quoting the Prophet: 'Permit women to come to mosques at night.' (Related by al-Bukhari) People say that the permission is given at night because the night provides additional cover and women are, thus, not seen by men.

In answer, we have the following points:

- Commenting on this hadith, Ibn Ḥajar said: 'The fact that the Prophet refers to permission at night means that they did not prevent them coming to the mosque during the day. The night is the time when suspicion may be aroused. Hence 'Abdullāh ibn 'Umar's son said: 'We do not give them permission so that they would not use it as a cover.' Al-Karmānī said: 'It may be suggested that special mention of permission at night means no permission during the day, while Friday Prayer is offered during the day. He responds to this saying that it should be understood as approving extension. If they are given permission to go at night, when the night raises suspicion, permission during the day is taken for granted. Some Ḥanafī scholars give the reverse argument, taking the hadith at its face value. They said that the night is mentioned in particular because sinners are busy with their sin at night, while during the day, they are at large. Although this is possible, the night is the time when suspicious behaviour is done. Moreover, not all sinners are busy at night. In most cases, the day gives them away if they harass women, because there are always people around. Whoever attempts what is unlawful is seen and censured.'
- It is very likely that women often used to ask permission to go to the night prayers, Fajr, Maghrib and 'Ishā', when the Qur'an is recited aloud. They wanted to listen to the Qur'an being recited by God's Messenger. The following texts confirm this:
    - 'Ā'ishah narrated: 'Believer women used to attend the Fajr Prayer with God's Messenger (peace be upon him).' (Related by al-Bukhari and Muslim)

- Umm al-Faḍl: 'This surah [Surah 77: Sent Forth] was the last I heard from God's Messenger as he recited it in Maghrib Prayer.' (Related by al-Bukhari and Muslim)
- 'Ā'ishah narrated: 'God's Messenger delayed the 'Ishā' Prayer until 'Umar called out to him saying: The women are dozing off.' (Related by al-Bukhari and Muslim)
- Ibn 'Umar narrated: 'One of 'Umar's wives used to attend the Fajr and 'Ishā' Prayers in the mosque with the congregation.' (Related by al-Bukhari)

Evidence 8

> Abu Hurayrah narrated: '... The best of men's rows is the first and the worst is the last, while of women's rows, the best is the last and the worst is the first.' (Related by Muslim)

Our opponents think that the hadith supports their view because it urges women to stay away from the men's rows. If this is urged in the mosque which inspires awe, and where men and women are preoccupied with their worship, it goes to reason that women should stay away from men's places in all areas of life outside the mosque.

We have the following three points in answer:

- The hadith mentions a particular type of manners related to congregational prayer. There are certain qualities that apply to assembling for prayer which are different from assembling for other purposes. For one thing, at the time of prayer, there is no conversation between the people present so that they need to be close in order to hear each other.
- At the time of worship, a person should be completely attentive to worship, thinking of nothing else, not even how to restrain

oneself from aspiring to some of what one desires. Widening the gap between men and women helps to concentrate on worship and the remembrance of God. On this point, al-Sarakhsī said: 'In prayer one is addressing God. One must not entertain anything that involves desire. When a man finds a woman next to him, such thoughts are normally present.'

- One thing that confirms the special case of such separation and its application only to congregational prayer is that when a woman prays in congregation with her father or brother or any other of her relatives that she cannot marry, i.e. *maḥrams*, she stands in a separate row, behind the rows of men.

Evidence 9

Abu Hurayrah narrated: 'Glorification is for men, but clapping is for women.' (Related by al-Bukhari and Muslim) Our opponents consider that the hadith shows that for a woman to speak aloud so as to be heard by men is forbidden or reprehensible.

In response, we say:

- The hadith mentions another aspect of manners that applies only during prayer, because worshippers must focus completely on their worship, removing all other thoughts or preoccupations, even making an effort not to be distracted by any potential temptation. We quoted al-Sarakhsī's statement that 'in prayer one is addressing God and one must not entertain anything that involves desire.' Ibn Ḥajar says: 'It appears that women are not meant to say a glorification aloud [to alert the imam to a mistake[2]] due to the fact that she is ordered to lower her voice in all situations in prayer, because of

2. A woman alerts the imam to a mistake by clapping.

the fear that she becomes a temptation.' The Qur'an teaches us the proper manners of conversation between men and women, telling the women: 'If you truly fear God, do not speak too soft, lest any who is sick at heart should be moved with desire.' (33: 32) Thus, good manners mean serious and properly considered speech, not withholding all sound so that men do not hear women. This means that we have two grades approved by Islam to prevent temptation. One is for all situations: 'Do not speak too softly', and the other is for congregational prayer, which is what this hadith mentions. We need to distinguish between what is special and what is general.

- The Sunnah shows us how women used to speak to men in all life situations, observing good manners. Many texts are provided in Volumes 2 and 3 of this abridged version.

Evidence 10

'Ā'ishah narrated: 'Had the Prophet seen what women have perpetrated, he would have stopped them, (in Muslim's version: he would have stopped them coming to the mosque) as the women of the Children of Israel were stopped.' (Related by al-Bukhari and Muslim) Our opponents consider the hadith as evidence to stop women coming to mosques.

Our answer makes several points:

- 'Ā'ishah said this when she saw some women doing what she did not approve of regarding wearing makeup and adornments. Hence, her words are understood as expressing disapproval and censure. They cannot be understood as akin to abrogation of the Prophet's order: 'Do not deprive women of their share of mosques.'

A fundamental principle of Islamic law is that its rulings cannot be abrogated by any person, regardless of that person's standing in knowledge, piety or companionship with the Prophet. In *al-Mudawwanah al-Kubrā* we read: 'I said: Did Mālik disapprove of women going to the mosque? He answered: As for going to mosques, Mālik used to say: "They may not be denied going to mosques."' Mālik was the Imam of Madinah nearly a hundred years after 'Ā'ishah made her statement. One type of evidence upheld by his school of Fiqh is the common practice of the people of Madinah.

☙ Scholars make good points in interpreting what 'Ā'ishah said. We sum it up as follows:

Ibn Ḥazm said: 'The Prophet did not see what they perpetrated, and therefore he did not stop them. Since he did not, then to stop them is wrong and a deviation... Whatever was perpetrated, it was undoubtedly done by some women, not all. It is impossible to deny what is good to people who did not perpetrate that just because others had perpetrated it...'

Ibn Qudāmah said: '... The Prophet's Sunnah is the one to follow. What 'Ā'ishah said applies to the ones who perpetrated whatever they did. For such a woman, going out is discouraged.'

Ibn Ḥajar said: '... Some uphold what 'A'ishah says to stop women coming to mosques in all cases, but this needs to be carefully considered. What she said cannot be the basis to change the ruling, because she attaches it to a condition which was not fulfilled, based on what she thought: 'Had he seen... he would have stopped them.' The response here is that he did not see and did not stop them. Therefore, the original ruling remains operative. Indeed, 'Ā'ishah did not specify stopping women going to the mosque, even though her words indicate that she felt they should be stopped. Moreover, God was fully aware of what women would perpetrate, but He did not instruct His Messenger to stop them. Had what women did required that they should be stopped from going to mosques, stopping them going to other places, such as the market place, would also have been required. Furthermore, the disapproved action was done by some women, not all of them. If anyone were to be stopped from going, it would have applied to those who so behaved. The better course is to consider what action would lead to something wrong and to stop it. This is what the Prophet (peace be upon him) indicated when he disallowed wearing perfume and adornments.'

'Abd al-Ḥamīd Ben Bādīs said: 'What 'Ā'ishah said is not contrary to the hadith quoted earlier, saying: "Do not prevent your women coming to mosques," because what those women perpetrated was wearing perfume and adornments. The Prophet (peace be upon him) ordered that women must not be stopped from going to mosques and he ordered women not to wear perfume when they wanted to go out. Had he seen what they perpetrated, he would have stopped them for having violated the condition, and they would be stopped until they abided by the condition. Thus, the stoppage would not mean an abrogation of his earlier order that women must not be prevented from going to mosques.'

Had 'Ā'ishah seen what women in our time do, going to all places of entertainment revealing parts of their bodies; had she witnessed what Muslim women are exposed to by the media which addresses them in their own homes and gains a hold on their minds and thoughts, and had she realized that the only places to which they do not go are mosques, what would she say? Would she have repeated her words or would she say: 'Had God's Messenger seen what women have perpetrated, he would have made it obligatory for them to go to mosques'? Just as she said her earlier words by way of censure, she would say this by way of encouragement and motivation, so that women would stay for some time away from the atmosphere of temptation and become familiar instead with values and propriety. Their hearts would, thus, feel humble at the remembrance of God, learn more about their faith and gain immunity from temptation.

To sum up, what is required is to prevent negative occurrences, so that what God has legislated remains in force.

Evidence 11

> 'Ā'ishah narrated: 'I said: "Messenger of God, does the duty of jihad apply to women?" He said: "Yes, they have a jihad in which no fighting takes place: the hajj and the 'umrah."' (Related by Ibn Mājah)

Our opponents cite this hadith as evidence confirming that Islam tends to prevent meeting between men and women. Despite the great merit of jihad, women have been kept away from it, simply because it does not fit with what is required of them of covering and staying away from men. They add that the fact that some female Companions of the Prophet joined him in the early expeditions was by force of necessity, given the number of men then available was small.

Several points may be raised in response:

- The hadith indicates the reason for not making jihad an obligatory duty on women. This reason is the 'fighting' which is contrary to the gentle nature of women. The Prophet says that their jihad is one 'in which no fighting takes place'. He did not say that in their jihad 'no mixing with men takes place'.

Besides, the hajj and the ʿumrah do not give women the sort of isolation they want to impose on them. During the hajj and the ʿumrah men and women are often together when they perform their rituals. Indeed, there is often overcrowding that exceeds what happens anywhere else.

- What necessity required that a small number of women accompany the Prophet on his expeditions, when a small number of old people or young lads who were not well trained to fight could have done the same work? Even if we accept that there was need for them to join the early expeditions because of the shortage of men, what need was there for them to join the later expeditions, such as those of Khaybar and Ḥunayn, when the number of men was much higher. Both al-Bukhari and Muslim relate hadiths indicating that Umm Sulaym took part in the Battle of Khaybar. Muslim also relates that Umm Sulaym was also with the Muslim army at the Battle of Ḥunayn. Ibn Saʿd mentions in *al-Ṭabaqāt al-Kubrā* that 15 Muslim women took part with the Muslim army at the Battle of Khaybar, and that Umm Sulayṭ was at the Battle of Ḥunayn.[3] Besides, what necessity required that Umm Ḥarām join the maritime expedition during Muʿāwiyah's reign, when Muslim armies had swept across vast areas and people had embraced Islam in large numbers? There was no reason for Umm Ḥarām to join that expedition except for the fact that God's Messenger prayed for her to be a martyr with those undertaking jihad at sea.
- The texts that mention women's participation in jihad often use the form 'it used to be' and 'we used to.' This provides strong evidence that such participation was the normal practice and continued over time. It was not the subject of any abrogation towards the end of the Prophet's life.

---

3. One line has been omitted here and some confusion occurs in this abridged version. I have included the missing line and corrected the text by reference to the unabridged work of the author.

Anas narrated: 'God's Messenger (peace be upon him) used to take Umm Sulaym and some women from the Anṣār on his expeditions.' (Related by Muslim) Al-Rubayyiʿ bint Muʿawwidh narrated: 'We used to go with the Prophet on his military expeditions to provide [the fighters] with drinking water and serve them.' (Related by al-Bukhari)

- If it is true that women were allowed to join jihad expeditions during the Prophet's lifetime because of necessity, would Ibn ʿAbbās be unaware of the fact? In response to questions put to him by Najdah of the Khawārij, Ibn ʿAbbās wrote: '... You wrote asking me whether God's Messenger (peace be upon him) used to take women with him on his expeditions? He certainly took women on jihad and they used to nurse the wounded and were given gifts from the war gains, but they were not given the full shares.' (Related by Muslim) Had necessity been the cause of taking women on jihad expeditions, Ibn ʿAbbās would have stated this because such explanation was obligatory so that the man would not misunderstand the matter.
- Both Ibn Baṭṭāl and Ibn Hajar state in their commentaries on al-Bukhari's *Ṣaḥīḥ*: 'Jihad is not obligatory on women in the same way as it is obligatory on men, but this does not mean that it is prohibited in their case. They may volunteer if they wish.'

Evidence 12

The hadith: 'A woman is *ʿawrah*: when she goes out, Satan receives her.' (Related by al-Tirmidhī)

Our response is in several points:

- If they claim that a woman may go out for a necessity; otherwise, her going out is forbidden or reprehensible, i.e. *makrūh*, we say: how can it be forbidden or reprehensible when the Prophet ordered men not to stop their women from going to pray in the mosque when prayer in the mosque is neither a necessity nor a need? On the other hand, they say that her going out for anything less than a necessity is contrary to what is preferable. In this case, we say how can it be so when the Prophet prayed for Umm Ḥarām to join the maritime expedition going on jihad, when her travel was neither a necessity nor a need. It was merely a voluntary action, seeking God's pleasure.

- As we confirm that for a woman to go out for something which is not a necessity, need or refinement is not forbidden, reprehensible or contrary to what is preferable, then what is the message of the hadith? The hadith links the woman's description as '*awrah* and her being received by Satan. The meaning, then, is a warning to the woman against being complacent in covering her '*awrah*. This means that when she goes out 'she must not reveal of her adornment anything other than what Islam permits, and she must not wear perfume, or walk or speak in a way that arouses temptation.' The hadith further warns the woman and the men around her against neglecting the values of propriety when she meets men, as these values ensure the covering of the '*awrah* and prevent attraction and temptation. Thus, Satan will be subdued and turn away.
- God's Messenger (peace be upon him) links women's going out with Satan in another hadith, saying: 'A woman comes in the image of a Satan and returns in the image of a Satan.' His expression, 'in the image of a Satan', is an expressive, figurative reference to the temptation associated with a woman coming towards a man or moving away from one. The way to overcome the temptation is pointed out by the Prophet as he continues the hadith: 'If any of you is attracted by a woman, he should go to his wife. That is certain to overcome what he feels.' This means that the answer is to strive against the attraction, lowering one's gaze whilst the

attractive woman is still around, then to go back to one's wife and find one's pleasure with her. Thus, the man suppresses the thoughts the Evil One tries to put in his mind. The solution is definitely not to keep women isolated at home, preventing them from going out. This is confirmed by countless cases we have mentioned about the woman's participation in social life during the Prophet's lifetime.

- The hadith warns us against the temptation presented by women, in the same way as other hadiths warn us against the temptation presented by wealth and children. This temptation is common, and God lets it operate so that He tests His servants. Every believer, man and woman, should approach life actively and seriously, so that they earn money and have children. They also meet as required by actively participating in a goodly and serious life. At the same time, they must guard against giving in to temptation.
- This hadith and similar ones that warn against the temptation of women and their going out are all singly-reported, which means that their authenticity is only 'probable', not confirmed. Moreover, their import is also of the 'probable' grade, which means that they admit more than one meaning. If they appear to be in conflict with other hadiths that are of confirmed authenticity and definite import which confirm women's participation in social life and all spheres of public and private life, as is clear from the hadiths quoted in Chapter 4 of Volume 2 of this abridged version, priority should be given to what is confirmed and definite. Indeed, what is probable should be interpreted in a way that makes it consistent with what is definite.

Evidence 13

A hadith runs as follows: 'God's Messenger said to his daughter Fāṭimah: "What is best for a woman?" She said:

"That she does not see a man and no man sees her." He embraced her and said: "[We are] the offspring of one another."'

Some of our opponents cite this hadith as confirming that the best option for any woman is to stay in her home and not to go out except twice: the first to go out of her father's home to her husband's home, and the second from her husband's home to the grave.

In response we say:

- This hadith is narrated with a chain of transmission that is lacking in authenticity. As such, it is unacceptable as evidence. In his grading of the hadiths quoted in al-Ghazālī's *Iḥyā' 'Ulūm al-Dīn*, al-Ḥāfiẓ al-'Irāqī says about it: 'It is related by al-Bazzār and in al-Dāraquṭnī's *al-Afrād* as narrated by 'Alī, with a chain of transmission that is authentically poor.' There is another version of it in *Majma' al-Zawā'id*, with a comment by al-Haythamī: 'Related by al-Bazzār and it includes one [i.e. a narrator] who is unknown to me.'
- This hadith contradicts hundreds of other hadiths which we have quoted from the authentic anthologies of al-Bukhari and Muslim. All of these quoted hadiths explain how Muslim women used to meet men during the Prophet's lifetime, when she saw them and they saw her. Who is more qualified to do what is 'best for a woman' – as alleged by this unauthentic hadith – than the Prophet's female Companions? It is sufficient to mention only the following Companions of the Prophet:
    - Umm al-Faḍl bint al-Ḥārith, the wife of the Prophet's uncle al-'Abbās: she embraced Islam about ten years before her husband, and she remained with the oppressed Muslims in Makkah until she migrated to Madinah with her husband after Makkah fell over to Islam.

- Umm Sulaym: the Prophet gave her the happy news that she was certain to be in heaven.
- Umm Ḥarām: the Prophet prayed for her to be a martyr.
- Asmā' bint 'Umays: who was married three times, and each one of her husbands was confirmed by the Prophet to be in heaven. Her first husband was Ja'far ibn Abi Ṭālib, then she married Abu Bakr, and her last husband was 'Alī ibn Abi Ṭālib.
- Asmā' bint Abu Bakr and the wife of al-Zubayr ibn al-'Awwām, the Prophet's close Companion.
- Su'ayrah al-Asadiyyah: the Prophet gave her the happy news that she would be in heaven.

☙ We have many authentic hadiths mentioning that Fāṭimah often went out of her home. If it is suggested that she was covered and men could not see her, she would still see them. However, in some of these hadiths it is clear that there was interchange between her and men. How can these authentic texts be viewed in the light of this hadith that is lacking in authenticity? Here are some of these texts.

> God says: 'If anyone should dispute with you about this [truth] after all the knowledge you have received, say: Come. Let us summon our sons and your sons, our women and your women, and ourselves and yourselves; then let us pray humbly and solemnly and invoke God's curse upon the ones who are telling a lie.' (3: 61) In his commentary on this verse, Ibn Kathīr said: 'This means bringing them so that they are present at the time of mutual prayer... The following morning, the Prophet came bringing al-Ḥasan and al-Ḥusayn [his two grandsons], while Fāṭimah walked just behind him to go ahead with the mutual prayer. At that time, he was married to several wives.'

- ‘Ā’ishah narrated: ‘Fāṭimah came walking: her walk was exactly the same as the Prophet’s walk. The Prophet said: “Welcome to my daughter.” He then sat her to his right.’ (Related by al-Bukhari and Muslim)
- ‘Ā’ishah narrated: ‘The Prophet came out one morning, covering himself with an untailored garment woven from black hair. Al-Ḥasan ibn ‘Alī came over and he took him under his garment, then al-Ḥusayn came and joined him. Then Fāṭimah came and he took her in, then ‘Alī came over and he took him in. He then said: “God only wants to remove all that is loathsome from you, you members of the [Prophet’s] household, and to purify you fully.”’ (33: 33) (Related by Muslim)
- Wāthilah ibn al-Asqa‘ narrated: ‘I went to see ‘Alī, but I did not find him. Fāṭimah said: “He has gone to invite God’s Messenger. Sit down.” He came accompanied by God’s Messenger. He entered and I entered with them. The Prophet called Ḥasan and Ḥusayn and sat each of them on his thigh and he drew Fāṭimah close to his lap, and did the same with her husband. He then brought his cloak over them all and said: “God only wants to remove all that is loathsome from you, you members of the [Prophet’s] household, and to purify you fully.”’ (33: 33) (Related by al-Bayhaqī)
- ‘Ā’ishah narrated: ‘The Prophet’s wives sent Fāṭimah, the Prophet’s daughter, to him. She sought permission to enter as he was reclining with me under my garment. He let her come in...’ (Related by Muslim)
- Al-Miswar ibn Makhramah narrated: ‘‘Alī proposed to marry Abu Jahl’s daughter. Fāṭimah was informed of this and she went to God’s Messenger (peace be upon him) and said: “Your people claim that you are not angered by what may be done to your daughters.”’ (Related by al-Bukhari and Muslim)

- Anas narrated: '... When God's Messenger was buried, Fāṭimah said: "Anas, were you happy to hurl dust over God's Messenger's body?"' (Related by al-Bukhari)
- 'Ā'ishah narrated: 'Fāṭimah and al-'Abbās came to Abu Bakr asking for their inheritance from God's Messenger (peace be upon him)...' (Related by al-Bukhari and Muslim)

- The hadith gives the impression that the screening, i.e. *ḥijāb*, which applied to the Prophet's wives in particular, requiring them to remain unseen by men inside their homes and not to go out except for real need, is also a duty or recommended for all Muslim women. Such a ruling is incorrect. We will discuss this issue of the Prophet's wives' screening in detail in Chapter 2.
- It is unfortunate that such a hadith, lacking authenticity as it is, is often quoted by speakers in Friday Prayers and it is mentioned in the books of some scholars. It is cited as if it is a divine directive given to Muslim women who aspire for perfection. What is worse is that some quote this hadith and then add: 'Related by the Four, and al-Tirmidhī grades it as "good, authentic."' 'The Four', in such context, refers to Abu Dāwūd, al-Tirmidhī, al-Nasā'ī and Ibn Mājah, who produced the four *Sunan* anthologies of hadith. The fact is that it is not mentioned at all in any of these four anthologies.

Evidence 14

Fāṭimah bint Qays reports that Abu 'Amr ibn Ḥafṣ divorced her three times... She came to the Prophet and told him. He said: 'He does not owe you maintenance.' He told her to stay with Umm Sharīk [during her waiting period]. He then told her: 'Umm Sharīk is frequently visited by my companions. Move to Ibn Umm Maktūm's home. As he is blind, you can remove your outer garments in his home.' In a different version: 'I dislike that your head cover may drop or your robe may be lifted and expose your legs, which lets people see of you what you dislike to be seen...' (Related by Muslim)

Our opponents say that God's Messenger ordered Fāṭimah not to stay at Umm Sharīk's place so that she would not mix with men.

The following points are given in answer:

- God's Messenger (peace be upon him) did not order Fāṭimah not to stay at Umm Sharīk's place in order to avoid meeting men. The meeting of men and women occurred there anyway between Umm Sharīk herself and other women of her family and her guests. Also, when Fāṭimah moved to Ibn Umm Maktūm's place, mixing took place there. The Prophet wanted to make things easy for Fāṭimah bint Qays, so that she would not have to put on her full garment and her head cover throughout the day, because men frequented Umm Sharīk's place at all times of the day. Therefore, the Prophet told her to go to Ibn Umm Maktūm's place who, being blind, would not see her when she took off some of her clothing. The whole point, then, is the woman's comfort and the Prophet's desire to make it easier for believers, as he was very compassionate. It has nothing to do with avoiding meeting men.
- There was no separation between Umm Sharīk's quarters and her guests' accommodation. Had there been a separation, the Prophet would not have told her: 'I dislike that your head cover may drop or your robe may be lifted and expose your legs, which lets people see of you what you dislike to be seen.' It was one house where men and women met. There was no harm in Fāṭimah bint Qays seeing Ibn Umm Maktūm or Umm Sharīk's guests seeing Fāṭimah and she seeing them. The difficulty was that she should would have to wear her full attire throughout the day.

Evidence 15

> Ibn ʿAbbās narrated: 'The Prophet took al-Faḍl ibn ʿAbbās behind him on his back on the Day of Sacrifice. Al-Faḍl was a smart young man. The Prophet stopped to answer people's questions. A pretty woman from [the tribe of] Khathʿam approached seeking God's Messenger's ruling. Al-Faḍl gazed at her, admiring her beauty. The Prophet turned back as al-Faḍl was looking at her. He put his hand back, held al-Faḍl's chin and turned his face so that he would not look at her.' (Related by al-Bukhari and Muslim)

Our opponents say that if God's Messenger turned al-Faḍl's face to the other side so that he would not look at the woman, who, then, can turn young men's faces so that they would not look at women participating in social life? Therefore, it is important to prevent participation and meetings.

We respond as follows:

- Lowering one's gaze is an Islamic manner which all Muslim men and women are ordered to observe. A Muslim strives to adhere to it. Sometimes he slips, and he will either remember, repent and seek God's forgiveness, or he will be reminded by others around him. Alternatively, his desire gets the better of him and he repeats his sinful action until God guides him to what is better.
- Since God's Messenger (peace be upon him) turned al-Faḍl's face to the other side, who turned the faces of others who were expected to do the same as al-Faḍl? Or was al-Faḍl ibn al-ʿAbbās – who was riding behind the Prophet on his camel – the only one among the pilgrims who yielded to Satan's promptings and committed such unlawful gazing?
- The hajj season is a good example of how men and women in Islamic society meet, without embarrassment, complication

> or adverse results, and how slips necessarily caused by the great overcrowding are overlooked. This hadith refers to the occasional slips that occur when men and women meet. Yet, God's Messenger did not feel that such slips justified issuing an order to women generally, and pretty ones in particular, to cover their faces. On the contrary, he said: 'A woman in consecration must not wear a veil or gloves.' (Related by al-Bukhari) Nor did he see it as justification to issue an order to women to steer away from places where men were gathered. Hence, he did not allocate time for women to do the *ṭawāf* on their own.

Finally, had women's participation in social life and their meeting with men often been a cause to let people's desires on the loose, God would not have permitted such participation and meeting in such a blessed season of worship as pilgrimage.

Three: Responses to Opponents' Arguments

Argument 1

> A sense of morality is a value to which Islam attaches high importance. When a woman participates in life activities alongside men, her chastity comes under some scrutiny.

We have the following points in response:

- All the measures of control Islam requires, whether in relation to what women may wear outside their homes, or to participation in social life alongside men, aim to enhance morality. Some may applaud this statement but at the same time forget that these measures are not enough, on their own, to achieve this goal. A fine sense of morality ensures that the human body, its beauty and desires, maintain their respectable status and are not looked at as cheaply attainable pleasure. Such a goal cannot be achieved through mere covering, whether through the cover of clothes or that of the walls of the woman's home.

Such coverage is only one essential factor but other factors are equally necessary for the achievement of the aforementioned goal. Foremost among these factors is the morality foundation, which is belief in God and the Last Day. Belief is not something suspended in mid-air or kept in a vacuum. Nor does it live in the human body. It settles in one's mind and heart. Therefore, allowing full opportunity for the mind to grow and for the heart to enhance its purity will strengthen faith. However, we must remember that interaction between these factors requires alert minds, where believing hearts and well covered bodies must remain active, so as to keep one on the path of faith. What must be considered, therefore, is how to ensure that a Muslim woman has certainty of faith at heart and clarity of mental vision so that her desire to maintain her chastity remains strong, unaffected by desire and temptation.

Undoubtedly, an alert mind and a devout heart will enhance a person's sense of propriety and morality. Likewise, upholding such values helps to maintain purity of heart and mind, as also physical strength and purity. A clear mind, reassured heart and strong body are all powers that God wants Muslims to use in building the best type of human life on earth. How can some believers realize that this sense of high morality enhances all these powers and then imagine that we, Muslims, try to suppress them and keep them inactive, unable to do the work God wants us to do? Some may say that there is ample space at home for a good use of all these powers and energies. Whilst this is certainly true, it is nonetheless not universally applicable. Looking after the family home and the upbringing of young children may take up all of a woman's time. Yet there are times when such duties take only a small portion of her time. In such a scenario, the woman will be in the unfortunate situation of plenty of spare time with little to do with it. It is this situation that is likely to lead to negative results. Thus, unless we use such energies, which our values and morality have enhanced for the benefit of the Muslim community, keeping the Muslim woman at home with little opportunity of any good action, will only transform this fine human being into nothing more than a miserable entity, replete with a feeble mind, stagnant heart and inactive body!

- An active sense of morality is one of the best qualities a person may have. It is essential and must not be undervalued or abandoned. However, its practical implementation does not have just one form that keeps women at home. It is subject to a variety of factors that are brought about by the social environment and the woman's circumstances. We need to look now at some examples from the life of the Prophet's female companions.

  - Sahl narrated: 'When Abu Usayd al-Sā'idī got married, he invited the Prophet and his companions. The one to cook their food and serve them was none other than his wife, Umm Usayd. She also soaked some dates in an earthenware jug the night before. When the Prophet finished eating, she blended the drink and served it to him.' (Related by al-Bukhari and Muslim)

    Is it not right to say that if the bride serves the guests invited to the wedding dinner while she is wearing decent and proper clothes, her action does not breach her sense of morality? Likewise, if she sits at home and has some legitimate fun with her friends, she maintains her sense of morality.
  - Asmā' bint Abu Bakr narrated: '... I used to carry the date stones on my head from al-Zubayr's [her husband] land... which the Prophet gifted to him. It was two miles away from where I lived. I was coming back one day, carrying the date stones on my head. I met the Prophet on his camel with a group of the Anṣār. He called me, and started to make his camel sit.

He wanted me to ride behind him. I felt too shy to be with all those men. I remembered that al-Zubayr was the most jealous of people...' (Related by al-Bukhari and Muslim)

Is it not to right to say that when a woman goes out, decently covered, to attend to some of her family's needs, she maintains her sense of morality, in the same way as when she stays at home because her husband or her servant spares her the need to go out?

- Ḥafṣah bint Sīrīn narrated: '... A woman came over and stopped at the palace belonging to Banī Khalaf. I visited her and she mentioned that her sister's husband was with the Prophet on twenty of his military expeditions. Her sister was with him on six of these expeditions. She said: 'We used to attend to those who were sick and treat the wounded.' (Related by al-Bukhari)
- Al-Rubayyiʿ bint Muʿawwidh narrated: 'We used to go with the Prophet on his military expeditions to provide [the fighters] with drinking water and serve them. We also returned the [bodies of the] killed ones to Madinah.' (Related by al-Bukhari)

Is it not right to say that if a woman maintains her decent appearance when she participates in jihad as suits her nature, she enhances her fine sense of morality, in the same way as one who stays at home, sewing outfits for the fighters?

As is clear from these examples, there are many different ways of implementation, yet the sense of morality remains firm and well observed.

Argument 2

> If it is permissible that men and women meet, such permissibility applies only in situations of necessity or need.

In answer we say:

- If we say that meeting between men and women is permissible only for a necessity or a need, this implies that it is forbidden in the first place because it is a necessity that relaxes a prohibition and makes what is forbidden permissible. Needs are treated in the same way as necessities. Such an assumption has no evidence from the Qur'an or the Sunnah. Indeed, the Sunnah is totally opposed to it, as we made clear in Chapter 4 of Volume 2 which is devoted to the 'participation of Muslim women in social life'.
- Some may say that a meeting between men and women is permissible only to serve some interest that is a necessity, need or improvement. The question here is: are we not narrowing down what God has left wide open? Whatever is made permissible aims to make things easier for people. Therefore, people do what is permissible or leave it in a natural way, without looking for a particular interest to serve by doing so. In other words, no person is questioned for doing, or failing to do, what is permissible. This is something God has left for His servants to choose. Therefore, when a meeting between men and women, which is permissible, takes place, there is no need to ask about the need for it or the interests it has served. This is only done when we want to determine whether a particular meeting is a duty or recommended, from the Islamic point of view. In rural society, participation and meeting between men and women are part of the ordinary pattern of daily life, due to the fact that women are very active, attending to a variety of tasks. A rural woman finds herself alone at home only for very limited and short periods. No one can say that this

pattern is contrary to the Shariah. Some women who are city dwellers are in a similar situation to rural women. Take for example the case of a headmistress of a girls' school, a nurse, or a medical doctor, or other professional women. They do tasks that require them to frequently meet men.

☙ The meeting of men and women may be forbidden or reprehensible at times, when Islamic manners and values are ignored. However, staying away may also be forbidden or reprehensible if it leads to the neglect of some duty or recommended matter. Likewise, if reasons requiring a meeting or staying away occur and a Muslim fails to do what is necessary, a verdict applies to that person according to the nature of the requirement. If it is a duty and one fails to do it, one commits what is forbidden. Reasons that make staying away include everything that must not be seen by men, such as exposure of charms, wearing revealing clothing and certain aspects of fun and play. Reasons that make a meeting recommended or a duty include the pursuit of knowledge, attending useful lectures, enjoining what is right and forbidding evil, providing assistance to a person in need, buying and selling, serving guests when men are not at home or unwell, etc. It is right to say that it is normal for a Muslim society to have varying measures of meeting and participation between men and women in order to facilitate life needs and ensure various interests. We discussed these in the first chapter of Volume 2. Likewise, in a Muslim society, there must be a measure of separation between men and women when there are reasons for such separation, as we mentioned earlier. Moreover, when Islamic manners are observed, they ensure moderation in mixed meetings so that they remain consistent with serious and virtuous life standards. Meeting with men lays certain burdens on women, such as wearing body-covering clothes, observing standards of decorum in conversation and movement, lowering one's gaze and guarding against temptation. As for the extent of meeting or staying away, this is left for Muslim individuals and Muslim society to decide. It differs for different people, societies and generations. The determining factors are what make life easier and what ensure the fulfilment of legitimate interests.

- Islamic manners apply to both meeting between men and women or staying away, whatever the respective conditions may be. We outlined the manners pertaining to mixed society in Chapter 2 of Volume 2 of this abridged version. Staying away also requires the observance of certain manners, including:

  - Lowering one's gaze, so that one does not stand at a window to look hard at people as they walk up and down. One should also not look hard at printed photos in magazines and other publications.
  - One should steer away from listening to profane jokes and stories.
  - Even when speaking from behind a screen, a woman should not soften her voice to give it an element of temptation.
  - One must keep away from indulging in sexual day dreaming.
  - All aspects of sexual misbehaviour should be avoided.

- Going out of one's way in order to meet people of the opposite sex is wrong and its opposite, going out of one's way to avoid such meetings, is also wrong. The first is the wrong way to satisfy desire, and the other involves a sort of indirect arousal of desire. It also causes unhealthy tension and sensitivity for both the man and woman, which may lead to an unhealthy mentality. God, the Wise who knows all, has given people an easy code of law which gives both man and woman a healthy and balanced mentality.
- God's Messenger always says the truth. He said: 'May God bestow mercy on a person who says something good and ensures a gain as a result, or refrains from saying something

evil, thus causing himself no harm.' Using the same pattern of speech, we may say: May God bestow mercy on a man and a woman who meet people of the opposite sex, in and for what is reasonable. They, thus, ensure a gain, or stay away from evil, causing themselves no harm.

Argument 3

People wonder: Is there really any serious meeting, with good aims, between men and women?

Perhaps it is not unreasonable to ask such a question. People find themselves facing two very hard alternatives: the first is a set of traditions that know nothing except total separation between men and women, and the woman's isolation from all spheres of life outside the home. Indeed, a Muslim woman is praised for not leaving her home except twice in her life: once to move from her father's home to her husband's home and the other from her husband's home to the grave. Such traditions also draw thick curtains across the woman's face, requiring the total concealment of her face, voice and even name. All such traditions are deviant, moving away from the Prophet's guidance. The second alternative is total mixing that sets no restriction as prevails in Western societies and which is advocated by some people who want to import that way of life into our Muslim societies. This is clearly erroneous and contrary to what God has legislated.

Struggling against inherited traditions on the one hand and loose Western morality on the other, these good people who are keen on good morality find themselves at a loss, as if choosing one or the other is inevitable. The strict attitude taken by the elders who want to stick to the old traditions and the opposite attitude taken by the younger generation can be seen within the framework of 'reaction', and reaction often takes man away from the right path, leading either to stringency or carelessness and irresponsibility.

Such a policy has led to a widening of the gap in the two attitudes. The elders say that a woman's true personality is reflected in her modesty, decency and honour. To preserve these she should stay at home all the time. The young respond by saying that the woman's personality is fulfilled when she is fully independent. Therefore, she must go out and experience life without any restriction. The elders say that the woman's responsibility is confined within her home, and she has nothing to do with anything outside it. The young retort that her responsibility is the same as man's responsibility. She must assume the same role in all spheres of life.

Thus, both hold to their extremist views, abandoning the moderate line which Islam requires of us in all aspects of life.

There is a better alternative that saves us from the strictness of the elders and the irresponsibility of the young and which dispenses with irrational reaction. This alternative has been available to man ever since the day God made His human creation into males and females, guiding man to enjoy what is permissible and refrain from what is forbidden. We find this alternative in the Qur'an, God's Book which we recite every day. One instance pointing to it is in the story of Moses when he saw the two young women unable to give water to their flock. God says:

> When he arrived at the wells of Madyan, he found there a large group of people drawing water [for their herds and flocks], and at some distance from them he found two women who were keeping back their flock. He asked them: 'What is the matter

> with you two?' They said: 'We cannot water [our animals] until the herdsmen drive home. Our father is a very old man.' So he watered their flock for them, and then he withdrew into the shade and prayed: 'My Lord! Truly am I in dire need of any good which You may send me.' One of the two women then came back to him, walking shyly, and said: 'My father invites you, so that he might duly reward you for having watered our flock for us.' And when [Moses] went to him and told him his story, he said: 'Have no fear. You are now safe from those wrongdoing folk.' (28: 23-25)

We see it also in the meeting between the Prophet Solomon and the Queen of Sheba when he invited her to believe in God's oneness. God says:

> She was told to enter the court. When she saw it, she thought it was a lake of water, and she bared her legs. Said he: 'It is but a court smoothly paved with glass!' She said: 'My Lord! I have indeed wronged my soul, but now I submit myself, with Solomon, to God, the Lord of all the worlds.' (27: 44)

We note the same alternative in all situations where men and women met during the Prophet's lifetime. Those mentioned in the two *Ṣaḥīḥ* anthologies of al-Bukhari and Muslim amount to nearly 300 cases.

The attitude of those who object to the line we are advocating is understandable. Theirs is a reaction to those who are fed up with inherited traditions and have broken away from them, and who have become captivated by Western values. In effect, they rejected one tradition only to embrace another. Instead, they should have reverted to the original guidance provided by Prophet Muhammad (peace be upon him).

- We would like to draw the reader's attention to a sort of psychological disorder which the late scholar Malek Bennabi called 'the psychosis of ease and psychosis of impossibility'. This disorder is reflected in a tendency to classify matters as either too easy or absolutely impossible, as if there is no situation which is 'difficult but possible'. Those who are prone to this disorder feel that the choice they have is either to follow their ancestors, which is easy for those who are religious, or to emulate the West, which is easy for those who wish to discard their values. If you speak to them about the society built by the Prophet and the community he established with his companions, they consider it an absolute impossibility in today's milieu. They see no way of applying the guidance provided by God and His Messenger to our contemporary life. We pray that God will spare us such a disorder, so that we see that the implementation of divine guidance is possible, even though it may be rather difficult. Its implementation requires: 1) God's help; 2) an initiative by leaders and reformers, and 3) a serious effort by the Muslim community. A good alternative is certainly necessary. It is not enough to denounce the lack of moral values in mixed society when this continues to be accelerating in our own society. Life has its own dictates, and contemporary life imposes different levels of mixing between men and women. Unless those who uphold Islamic values come forward and present the good example that will suit every Muslim who is keen to adhere to proper morality, which ensures that meetings between men and women are both moral and serious, then the erring trend will sweep all before it.
- May I remind all those who are keen on morality of what Shaykh Nāṣir al-Dīn al-Albānī wrote in the Introduction to his book *Ḥijāb al-Mar'ah al-Muslimah* [i.e. The attire of the Muslim woman] commenting on the permissibility of uncovering women's faces. He wrote:

> My heart is in absolute grief at what we see of total disregard to values of propriety and decorum as women in our time go further into it, without check. However, I do not consider that the way to deal with it is to forbid what God has made lawful or permissible. Since God has permitted women to keep their faces uncovered, it is not for us to impose on them that they should totally cover their faces, without relying on a clear command by God and His Messenger. Indeed, the purpose of divine legislation, its gradual approach and some of its fundamental principles including the Prophet's order: 'Make things easy, not difficult', as well as the sound principles of education and discipline: all these combine to put scholars and guides of the Muslim community under a clear obligation. They must approach women gently, treat them kindly and allow them what God has made permissible.

A gentle approach to people, giving them the easier option and making easy what God has permitted all constitute the better alternative which we must put into practice, so that people will adopt it. This approach is useful in societies where unrestricted mixing has become widely spread. It is certainly very effective with people who still retain a wish for an easy and virtuous life. It is our belief that not everyone who has gone with the new trend embraces Western permissive philosophy; rather, many of those who maintain a good religious sense have been overcome by this powerful trend of change, and they are in need of a helping hand to save themselves.

Offering a sound alternative is also useful in conservative societies where the Westernization trend is only resisted by the mere clinging to traditions and denunciation of new ideas and practices. Experience in many countries shows that this approach cannot withstand the forceful trend of Westernization. It is clear that we need a new standpoint, relying on the Prophet's guidance in order to hold its own. Should such an attitude be adopted in conservative societies, it will be certain to foil all the attempts of change those whose eyes have been dazzled by the appeal of the Western way of life continue to make.

☙ We may also say to those who are keen to preserve moral values that the only way to appreciate the meaning and significance of women's participation in social life is to revise our attitude towards women and adopt the view expressed by God's Messenger as he says: 'Women are the full sisters of men.' (Related by Abu Dāwūd) Every woman is an honoured human being. Man's attitude to her is in no way the same as his attitude to a sex game. It is a relation between two human beings who share human life that combines all aspects of an honourable and virtuous life. This permeates everything in life: ideas, concepts, feelings, emotions, as well as social, economic and political activities. As this joint life cannot be divorced from the natural tendency towards the opposite sex, Islam puts in place a set of values and manners to keep this tendency on the right track and which allows life to progress in a clean and good way.

☙ To sum up: traditions have been unfair to the Muslim woman, denying her a full chance of participation in social life, using religion as a pretext. This is, in fact, unfair to religion, resulting in neglecting and wasting several legitimate interests. The inability to look at the Islamic justification of women's participation in social life and the legitimate channels of such participation has resulted in people using illegitimate channels at times and allowing participation that was heedless of Islamic manners at other times. This is because there was need for such participation on the one hand yet our societies were under intellectual pressure on the other. Therefore, it is essential that we look at Islam and determine the extent of women's participation in social life so that such participation can be set on the right course and is shown to be sanctioned by Islam.

Argument 4

People say that when the natures of man and woman meet, they are bound to have the same attraction and pleasant company that exists between men and women. One evil will lead to another. Therefore, it is better, wiser and more effective to shut the door completely.

- The premise of natural attraction and pleasant company is certainly true, as God has given us our nature. The question we ask in response is: why, then, did God and His Messenger open the way for women's full participation in all public and private areas of social life, as explained in Chapter 4 of Volume 2? This can only be for a very important purpose.
- A certain measure of attraction and pleasant company occurs naturally when man meets woman. In other words, it occurs unintentionally because it is part of human nature. If they do not allow this mutual attraction to run its course, focusing their attention on the serious matter that has brought them together, there is no harm in their meeting. This means that they only have to ensure that their feelings are kept under control, and they focus on how to achieve the purpose of their meeting.
- What happens of mutual attraction and pleasant feeling at the outset, followed by a control of feelings and serious attention to the matter in hand is the same as what happens at first sight and the pleasant feeling it generates. When one of his companions asked him about a man's spontaneous

look at a woman, the Prophet answered: 'Turn your sight away.' He told another: 'The first glance is yours, but not the later one.' Thus, we see that God tests men and women by the first and spontaneous glance. He has not closed all possibilities to it by making it obligatory for women to cover their faces. Likewise, He tests them with the initial feelings of attraction when man meets woman, but He does not close all possibilities for such feeling by prohibiting all meetings and participation. We must not forget that by such testing, God wants to make things easier for men and women believers to serve their legitimate interests and to build life on earth in the purest and most perfect model.

- Is it really better, wiser and more effective to shut the door completely to prevent any chance of immorality? In answer, we refer the reader to Volume 6 of this abridged version, as it is dedicated to the discussion of the exaggerated use of the rule of 'preventing the cause'. We only need to remember here what Ibn al-'Arabī said in his book *al-Aḥkām*: '... In every risky matter where God entrusts people to their honest behaviour, we may not say: it can be used to justify what is forbidden; therefore, it must be prevented.' In his annotations of al-Shāṭibī's *al-Muwāfaqāt*, the late Shaykh 'Abdullāh Draz says: 'God attaches many obligations to a person's honesty and diligence. As such, we may not attach to it more stringent controls so as to prevent causes and guard against their becoming widespread.'
- We remind our opponents of the fact that they take the opposite view on a different matter. They are told that times have gone bad and morality has weakened. People are resorting to divorce and polygamy too easily, paying little or no attention to Islamic controls. Therefore, it is necessary to ban or restrict divorce and polygamy. When our opponents are faced with this argument, they retort: how can we ban what God has made permissible? How can we restrict what

God has made available and open to people? They further say that such flaws and defects cannot be addressed by banning or imposing restrictions, but rather by proper education and admonition. The question we put to them is: why do we not apply the same solution to mixing and participation between men and women? Why do they want to impose a strict prohibition on mixing and participation and on uncovering women's faces as the pretext of times changing for the worse and morality weakening? Why do they not address this situation instead with education and admonition?

God has made divorce and polygamy lawful, as He did in permitting women to uncover their faces and participate in social life. To ban divorce and polygamy or restrict them will present difficulties for people. Likewise, imposing orders to cover women's faces and stop their participation in social life will present difficulties.

It is far better and more sound to apply God's law as it is. Addressing faults through education and admonition while only moderately using the method of cause prevention is certainly better and wiser.

Argument 5

Our highly respected scholars were not unaware of the texts that permit meeting between men and women, but they realized that times had changed for the worse which led them to restrict what was allowed during the time of the Prophet (peace be upon him) and his exemplary companions. Further, we believe that the real reason for raising this subject at this present time is that people are dazzled by what they see in Western societies of women mixing with men in all spheres of life.

In response we have the following to say:

- We share with them the great respect due to our earlier scholars. There is no doubt that like all generations that benefited by their learning, we are greatly indebted to them. It is to their credit that they did not deny anyone, whether their contemporary or those belonging to a later generation, the right to differ with them. The only criterion to be applied in this regard is the provision of evidence from God's Book and the Prophet's Sunnah. As for the views of others, they are included in what Imam Mālik said: 'You may take or reject from anyone's views, except from the one in this grave [pointing to the Prophet's grave].'
- As for the argument of times changing for the worse, leading to restricting what was permitted during the Prophet's lifetime, this will be fully answered in Volume 6 of this abridged version.
- As for being 'dazzled' by what we see in Western societies, well; it is God alone who knows what is in people's hearts. Is it that they are dazzled by Western civilization or are they profoundly motivated by their knowledge of the Prophet's Sunnah? As Western civilization is mentioned, we wish to quote these fine words by Imam Ibn Taymiyyah: 'We are prohibited from imitating the people of other religions in what was not part of the practice of the early generations of the Muslim community. What early Muslims practised, whether by omission or commission, is fine. We do not abandon what God requires us to do only because unbelievers do it. However, God has not given us an order with which they agree without including in it some differences that distinguish the true divine faith from what was altered or abrogated.'

Imam Ibn Taymiyyah tells the truth: there is always a difference that distinguishes the divine faith. Islam lays down a set of fine manners which distinguish a Muslim woman's participation in social life from the participation of Western women.

Argument 6

> There are many texts which scholars say allow meetings between men and women, but they qualify this by saying that they were, or might have been, revealed before the legislation of the *ḥijāb*.

This argument is often cited in order to bypass the rulings of many texts. Therefore, we will prove in the next chapter that the *ḥijāb* applied only to the Prophet's wives and cannot be extended to other Muslim women.

Argument 7

> There are many texts which scholars say allow meetings between men and women. Nevertheless, and considering how far the change for the worse has gone, they prefer to prohibit such meetings on the basis of preventing the cause.

This argument is often cited to bypass many texts and their rulings. We will devote Volume 6 of this abridged series to a detailed discussion of the rule that permits the prohibition of the cause and how far it has been exaggerated.

CHAPTER II

The Debate: The *ḥijāb* Requirement Applied Only to the Prophet's Wives

- Foreword
- Scholars' Statements Concerning the Hijab and its Being Applicable Only to the Prophet's Wives
- The Applicability of the Hijab in the Light of the Fundamental Principles of Jurisprudence

We mentioned in the previous chapter that people argue that the numerous hadith texts mentioning cases of meetings between men and women probably refer to events that took place prior to the revelation of the Qur'anic verse stating the *ḥijāb* requirement. This argument is often cited in order to bypass the rulings of many texts. Therefore, we will devote the present chapter to proofs that the *ḥijāb* applied only to the Prophet's wives. When we take this into account, the whole argument based on this verse collapses.

Foreword

One: Definition of *ḥijāb*

The relevant Qur'anic verse says: 'When you ask them for something, do so from behind a *ḥijāb*.' (33: 53) This means that the woman concerned sits or stands behind something that screens her. The statement does not refer to any sort of garment she wears to cover her body. The implementation of this order means that when men spoke to the Prophet's wives they did so from behind a screen, so that they did not see them. They were permitted to go out for their needs, but when they did so they were to cover their faces in addition to covering their bodies. Thus, the essential meaning is that the Prophet's wives were not allowed to meet men who were not related to them without having a cover shielding them so that men did not see them. They were required to cover all their bodies when they went out as an alternative to having a screen. Thus, the *ḥijāb* took two forms: a standard one inside the home which required them to be screened when they talked to men who were unrelated to them, and a secondary one for outside, which meant that they had to cover their faces in addition to covering their bodies. In this chapter, we are concentrating on the discussion of the standard form because it is closely related to meetings between men and women. The other form will be further discussed within the context of the permissibility of uncovering women's faces. We have the following evidence endorsing what we say: that the essential meaning of the *ḥijāb* was and is screening the Prophet's wives.

From the Qur'an

The first endorsement is in the same verse: 'When you ask the Prophet's wives for something, do so from behind a *ḥijāb*: this makes for greater purity for your hearts and theirs.' The verse clearly states that the question and the answer are given from behind a *ḥijāb*, i.e. a screen, which by nature shields people. The verse then adds: 'This makes for greater purity for your hearts and theirs.' This means that 'to ask them from behind a screen' gives your hearts greater purity as you do not see them, and it also gives greater purity to their hearts as they do not see you. This cannot be achieved unless the people themselves are screened. Covering their bodies only does not fulfil the same requirement. It prevents men from seeing the women, but it does not prevent the women from seeing the men. Stating this meaning of the verse, al-Ṭabarī says in his commentary: 'This makes for greater purity for your hearts and theirs from what may occur within men's hearts in respect of women, through looking with their eyes, and what may occur within women's hearts in respect of men. It ensures that Satan has no way to get to you or to them.'

From the Sunnah

- Anas ibn Mālik narrated: 'I am the one who knows about this verse (ordering the *ḥijāb*) best. When Zaynab bint Jaḥsh was wed to God's Messenger (peace be upon him), she was with him at home. He prepared food and invited people. They sat conversing. (In Muslim's version: His wife turned her face to the wall.) The Prophet went out and came back more than once while the people continued in their conversation. God then revealed the verse related to the *ḥijāb*... Thus the screening was ordered. The people left.' (Related by al-Bukhari and Muslim)

Had the *ḥijāb* meant covering the body, and Zaynab, his bride, was sitting with her face to the wall but her face was uncovered, the Prophet would simply have told her to cover her face. There would have been no need to drop the curtain and prevent Anas's entry.

- 'Ā'ishah narrated: '... God's Messenger (peace be upon him) drew lots between us as he was about to go on a military expedition. It came out in my favour. I went with God's Messenger (peace be upon him) after the screening was made obligatory. I was carried and put down in my howdah...' (Related by al-Bukhari and Muslim)

'Ā'ishah mentions that she was carried in her howdah. This gives us the impression that even when travelling, the Prophet's wives were screened as far as possible. They should not to be seen, even covered, except when there was clear need that made screening impossible.

- Anas narrated: 'The Prophet stopped three days between Khaybar and Madinah so as to have his wedding with Ṣafiyyah bint Ḥuyay... Some Muslims said: "She is either one of the Mothers of the Believers, or she is one his right hand possesses [i.e. a slave]." Then they said: "If he screens her, she is a Mother of the Believers, but if he does not, she is one he possesses." When he was about to leave, he prepared her place behind him [on his mount] and put a screen between her and the people.' (Related by al-Bukhari and Muslim)

In this case, Ṣafiyyah came out and rode while the Prophet's Companions were looking. Needless to say, she was well covered. So why would they say: 'If he screens her, she is a Mother of the Believers'? Why would the Prophet 'put a screen between her and the people' if the *ḥijāb*, as mentioned in this verse, meant nothing more than covering the woman's body?

In our perusal of the majority of hadith anthologies, hadith by hadith, we have not seen a single hadith which refers to covering the body rather than the person. Indeed, every hadith we have examined confirms that the *ḥijāb* means the screen that separates the places of men and women, and that it denotes shielding the person, not the body.

Scholars' views

- Commenting on the verse that says: 'When you ask them for something, do so from behind a *ḥijāb*', al-Baghawī says: 'It means: from behind a screen. When this verse was revealed, it was no longer permissible for anyone to look at a wife of God's Messenger (peace be upon him) whether she was wearing a veil or not.'
- Ibn Qutaybah said: 'If Mothers of the Believers left their homes, to perform the hajj, or for some other duty, or for any need that required their going out, the obligation of screening was not enforced, because no one would enter their places during travel. As they were on their travels, they would be seen. The obligation applied only in the places where they would be staying.'
- *Qadi* 'Iyāḍ said: 'It was not permissible for the Mothers of the Believers to show themselves even though they were well covered, except when they had to go out to answer the call of nature. When they narrated hadiths, they would sit behind a screen. If they went out, they would be completely covered.'

Two: The date of the revelation

Most probably, the verse stating the obligation of screening was the month of Dhul-Qaʿdah in the fifth year of the Prophet's migration to Madinah, as stated by Ibn Saʿd, the author of *al-Ṭabaqāt al-Kubrā*.

The Evidence Confirming the Specific Applicability of the ḥijāb

Evidence 1: The Qur'anic verse

God says: 'Believers! Do not enter the Prophet's homes, unless you are given leave, for a meal without waiting for its proper time. But when you are invited, enter; and when you have eaten, disperse without lingering for the sake of mere talk. Such behaviour might give offence to the Prophet, and yet he might feel too shy to bid you go. God does not shy of stating what is right. When you ask the Prophet's wives for something, do so from behind a screen: this makes for greater purity for your hearts and theirs. Moreover, it does not behove you to give offence to God's Messenger, just as it would not behove you ever to marry his widows after he has passed away. That is certainly an enormity in God's sight.' (33: 53)

The verse expressly mentions the Prophet's homes and wives, and does not mention the homes and wives of other Muslims. In his *al-Fatāwā*, Ibn Taymiyyah says: 'The pronoun in the sentence, "When you ask them for something...," refers specifically to his wives. There is no mention of slave women in the whole address.' We add: Nor is there any mention of the wives of ordinary Muslim men.

In his commentary on the Qur'an, Imam al-Ṭabarī speaks about the verse that says: 'It is no sin for them [to appear freely] before their fathers, their sons, their brothers, their brothers' sons, their sisters' sons, their womenfolk, or such men slaves as their right hands possess. [Wives of the Prophet!] Always remain God-fearing; for God is witness to all things.' (33: 55) 'God, the Exalted, says that there is no harm or sin that applies to the Prophet's wives concerning their fathers. Scholars differ concerning what the verse refers to as it says there is no sin that applies to the Prophet's wives in regard to those named. Some say that they commit no sin if they remove their outer garments in their homes, while others say that they commit no sin if they do not stay behind a screen when they are with them.... The view that is closer to the truth is that they committed no sin if they did not screen themselves from the named close relatives. This verse is very close to the one that places the obligation of screening on the Prophet's wives.'

We note that God makes an exception to the immediate relatives of the Prophet's wives from the requirement of screening, as he says: 'It is no sin for them to appear before their fathers, their sons, their brothers...' Contrast this with the exception He makes in the case of the immediate relatives of Muslim women generally: 'Let them draw their head-coverings over their bosoms and not display their charms to any but their husbands, or their fathers, or their husbands' fathers...' (24: 31) Here the exception relates to displaying their charms and adornments which applies to all women. Further confirmation that this verse proves the applicability of the *ḥijāb* only to the Prophet's wives is seen in the fact that this verse mentions 'their husbands' while the verse mentioning the *ḥijāb* does not. This is because the verse in Surah 24 addresses all Muslim women, and each of them has a husband. The verse stating the requirement of the *ḥijāb* does not because it applied only to the Mothers of the Believers, and they all had one well-known husband, the Prophet (peace be upon him).

Evidence 2: Preliminaries to the *ḥijāb* obligation

- *'Umar suggests screening the Prophet's wives*

  'Umar narrated: '... I said: Messenger of God, [all sorts of people] pious and non-pious enter your homes. Perhaps you may wish to order the Mothers of the Believers to be screened. God subsequently revealed the verse of the *ḥijāb*.' (Related by al-Bukhari)

  The hadith specifically states that 'Umar advised the Prophet to screen his wives, but he did not say to him: 'Order believing women to be screened.' What happened was that 'Umar disliked all sorts of people being able to see the Prophet's wives, as they came in. Needless to say, as the Prophet was required to explain the faith to all people, his home should be open to whoever wished to see him. The homes of ordinary Muslims are normally frequented by relatives and friends and these are well trusted.

- *'Umar declares his recognition of Sawdah as she went out at night*

  'Ā'ishah narrated that 'the Prophet's wives used to go to al-Manāṣi', which is a wide area with no vegetation, to relieve themselves. 'Umar used to counsel the Prophet to screen his wives, but the Prophet did not do so. One night, Sawdah bint Zam'ah, the Prophet's wife, went out after 'Isha. She was a tall woman. 'Umar called out to her: "We recognize you, Sawdah." He said this because he was keen that we should be screened. God then revealed the *ḥijāb* obligation.' (Related by al-Bukhari and Muslim)

What 'Umar wanted was not the screening of all Muslim women; his concern extended only to the Prophet's wives. This is confirmed by Imam al-Nawawī as he says: 'The hadith implies alerting noble people and those in high position to what serves their own interests and giving them counsel, and also to repeating this when necessary.' We need only to think of the way al-Nawawī expresses this: 'alerting noble people and those in high position to what serves their interest.' He makes clear that these are their own private interests, not the interests of the Muslim population generally.

- *The Prophet's inconvenience as people stayed talking after the meal*

Anas ibn Mālik narrated: 'When Zaynab bint Jaḥsh was wed to God's Messenger (peace be upon him), she was with him at home. He prepared food and invited people. They sat conversing. The Prophet went out and came back more than once while the people continued in their conversation. God then revealed the verse related to the *ḥijāb*...' (Related by al-Bukhari and Muslim)

Imam Ibn Ḥajar said: 'Mujāhid narrated from 'Ā'ishah a different reason for the revelation of the *ḥijāb* verse. This is related by al-Nasā'ī as follows: 'The Prophet and I were eating *ḥays* served in a wooden plate when 'Umar passed by. The Prophet invited him. [As we were eating], his finger touched mine. He said: "Ah! Had he listened to my advice concerning you, no one would set an eye on any of you. The *ḥijāb* obligation was revealed.' In his commentary on the Qur'an, Ibn Jarīr al-Ṭabarī narrated through Mujāhid: 'As the Prophet was eating with some of his companions, and 'Ā'ishah was eating with them, one man's hand touched her hand. The Prophet disliked this, and the *ḥijāb* verse was then revealed.'

Ibn Mardawayh related a hadith as narrated by Ibn 'Abbās: 'A man entered the Prophet's home and stayed long. The Prophet went out [and returned] three times so that the man would leave, but he did not. ‘Umar came in and he noticed that the Prophet looked displeased. He said [to the man]: “Perhaps you have inconvenienced the Prophet.” The Prophet [later] said [to ‘Umar]: “I went out three times so that he would follow me, but he did not.” ‘Umar said: “Messenger of God, perhaps you should put up a screen. Your wives are unlike other women, and it would make for greater purity for their hearts.” The *ḥijāb* verse was subsequently revealed.’

There is no harm in there being several incidents suggesting the need for revelation. In the present case, the reports are reconciled by saying that such incidents took place, showing the need for legislation on this point. The last was the situation pertaining to Zaynab bint Jaḥsh, the Prophet’s wife, because the verse refers to that occasion.

- *‘Umar’s initiatives and their significance in connection with the* ḥijāb

    1. ‘Umar said: ‘I tallied with God, or my Lord tallied with me, on three matters. I said: Messenger of God, you may wish to make Maqām Ibrāhīm [i.e. the place where Abraham stood] a place of prayer. And I said: Messenger of God, [all sorts of people] pious and non-pious enter your homes. Perhaps you may wish to order the Mothers of the Believers to be screened. God subsequently revealed the verse of the *ḥijāb*. I was informed that the Prophet remonstrated with some of his wives. I went to see them. I said to them: You shall desist or God will give His Messenger wives who are better than you. I saw one of his wives and she said to me: “Has God’s Messenger nothing to say to admonish his wives, so that you are now admonishing them?” God then revealed the verse that says: “Were he to divorce you, his Lord may well give him in your stead spouses better than you: women who surrender themselves to God.”’ (66: 5)

2. ʿUmar ibn al-Khaṭṭāb narrated: '... When they took those captives [in the Battle of Badr], God's Messenger (peace be upon him) said to Abu Bakr and ʿUmar: "What do you think we should do about these captives?" Abu Bakr said: "Messenger of God, these are our cousins and clansmen. I think you should take ransom from them which will strengthen us against the unbelievers. It may be that God will later guide them to Islam." The Prophet said: "And what do you think, Ibn al-Khaṭṭāb?" I said: "No, by God! I do not share Abu Bakr's view. I would rather you instruct us and we strike their necks..." God's Messenger (peace be upon him) liked what Abu Bakr said and disliked what I said. On the morrow, I went over and I found God's Messenger and Abu Bakr seated and both were weeping... God, the Mighty and Exalted, revealed: "It does not behove a Prophet to have captives unless he has battled strenuously in the land."' (8: 67) (Related by Muslim)
3. Ibn ʿUmar narrated: 'When ʿAbdullāh ibn Ubay died, his son ʿAbdullāh ibn ʿAbdullāh came to see the Prophet and requested that he give him his shirt to wrap his father's body with. The Prophet gave him it. He then requested that he offer the funeral prayer for him. God's Messenger stood up to offer the prayer. ʿUmar stood up and held the Prophet's robe. He said: "Messenger of God, will you pray for him when God has forbidden you to do so?" God's Messenger said: "God has given me a choice, saying: 'You may pray for their forgiveness or may not pray for them, [for it will all be the same]. Even if you were to pray seventy times for their forgiveness, God will not forgive them' (9: 80). I shall do more than seventy times." ʿUmar said: "He was a hypocrite." God's Messenger offered the funeral prayer for him, and God revealed: "You shall not pray for any of them who dies, and you shall not stand by his grave" (9: 84).' (Related by al-Bukhari)

The quoted texts show that three of 'Umar's initiatives were related to public matters of the Muslim community. These were the ones concerning making Maqām Ibrāhīm a place of prayer, the captives in the Battle of Badr and offering the funeral prayer for hypocrites. The fourth initiative concerned his advice to the Prophet's wives, one of whom was his own daughter, Ḥafṣah. The initiative concerning the *ḥijāb* pertained to the Prophet's own private affairs. It was normal that the Prophet should put in place a system and arrangement that ensured his wives' modesty and chastity while remaining consistent with a man's feelings of privacy and honourable jealousy. This should be done without any difficulty and without awaiting revelations or advice by someone else, in this case 'Umar. The question is: why then did the Prophet not take the necessary action to screen his wives if their continued appearance was contrary to modesty and chastity? Moreover, why did he not act immediately on 'Umar's suggestion?

The answer is that the Prophet did not consider interaction between men and women, within the normal standards of propriety, to be contrary to man's integrity, morality and the preservation of family honour. This while he says: 'Do you wonder at Sa'd's jealous protectiveness? By God I am more jealously protective than him, and God is even more protective than myself.' (Related by Muslim) Nor did he consider it contrary to the woman's honourable behaviour or her modesty. In other words, the Prophet considered that the social traditions upheld in Madinah at the time were good and did not need to be contradicted. Nor did the Prophet see women's screening in all situations as a good thing for women. What was good for a Muslim woman was to dress decently, wear her head cover and a dress that covered her whole body, as God required of Muslim women. 'Umar, on the other hand, noticed that all sorts of people came into the Prophet's homes. At the same time, he felt that the Prophet's wives should be distinct from Muslim women generally. Hence, his insistence that they should be so. The Prophet, however, did not take up his advice because he disliked being in a position of distinction among his companions. Then there came a time when inconvenience to the Prophet became more frequent and needs for distinction became more pressing. Houses were small and entering the Prophet's homes, which was done very frequently because of people's different needs, meant seeing his wives, let alone staying long and engaging in pleasant conversation. All this could cause inconvenience or embarrassment to the whole family. This was particularly the case on the day following Zaynab's wedding.

The worst of all these incidents was when one person impudently declared his intention to marry one of the Prophet's wives after he died. God declared the Prophet's wives as Mothers of the Believers, which was a gesture of honour to His beloved Messenger. Therefore, God willed to stop all aspects that upset the Prophet and to protect his home. Indeed, He willed to elevate the Prophet's home to a status that was clearly above that of all believers' homes. He, therefore, revealed one verse outlining all the manners He wanted Muslims to observe:

i. Do not enter the Prophet's homes, unless you are given leave, for a meal without waiting for its proper time.
ii. But when you are invited, enter; and when you have eaten, disperse without lingering for the sake of mere talk.
iii. When you ask the Prophet's wives for something, do so from behind a screen: this makes for greater purity for your hearts and theirs.
iv. It does not behove you to give offence to God's Messenger, just as it would not behove you ever to marry his widows after he has passed away. That is certainly an enormity in God's sight. (33: 53)

We conclude our comment on 'Umar's initiatives by the following observations.

First, ʻUmar was known to be very jealously protective. This is confirmed in two hadiths. Ibn ʻUmar narrated: ʻOne of ʻUmar's wives regularly attended the Fajr and ʻIsha prayers with the congregation at the mosque. She was asked: "Why do you come out for these prayers when you know that ʻUmar dislikes this and is jealous?" She said: "Why does he not stop me?" They said: "He is prevented by the Prophet's order: ʻDo not stop women servants of God from attending God's mosques.'"' (Related by al-Bukhari)

Abu Hurayrah narrated: ʻAs we were sitting at God's Messenger's, he said: "As I was asleep, I saw myself in heaven. I saw a woman performing *wudu* beside a palace. I asked whose palace it was. They said that it belongs to ʻUmar ibn al-Khaṭṭāb. I remembered how jealous he was and I turned away from it." ʻUmar wept and said: "Would I be jealous of you, Messenger of God?"' (Related by al-Bukhari and Muslim)

Secondly, the Prophet's protectiveness was healthy, attaining the degree of perfect soundness that fit with his perfect manners and standards.

Thirdly, the Prophet's sound protectiveness accepted that his wives remained unscreened until he received revelations that removed all aspects of inconvenience from him and elevated the status of his homes. It also accepted that Muslim women generally remained unscreened. The Prophet continued to see and mix with Muslim women on different occasions, together with his Companions. Bearing this in mind, we can say that meetings between men and women, without a separating screen, for all legitimate purposes, is permissible unless something occurs to alter the original permissible status and make it reprehensible, i.e. *makrūh*, of either the mild or strong degree.

Evidence 3: After the *ḥijāb* obligation

'Umar expressed his disapproval when he saw Sawdah, the Prophet's wife, going out after the order to screen the Prophet's wives was revealed. 'Ā'ishah narrated: 'One day after the *ḥijāb* order was given, Sawdah went out for her need. She was a big woman who would be recognized by anyone who knew her. 'Umar ibn al-Khaṭṭāb saw her and said: 'Sawdah, you cannot be unrecognized by us. Therefore, consider how you go out.' She immediately went back. God's Messenger was in my home, having his dinner and he held a bone with some meat. She came in and said: "Messenger of God, I went out to relieve myself and 'Umar said this and that to me." He received revelations and it was soon over, with the bone remaining in his hand. He did not put it down. He said to her: "You [meaning his wives] are permitted to go out to relieve yourselves."' (Related by al-Bukhari and Muslim)

'Umar did not object to Muslim women going out to relieve themselves after the revelation of the *ḥijāb* verse. They all went out, as there were no toilets at anyone's home. Moreover, many women went out for different purposes. He only objected to Sawdah, the Prophet's wife, because he was aware that the *ḥijāb* applied only to the Prophet's wives. Imam Ibn Ḥajar quotes al-Qurṭubī: ''Umar disliked that anyone should see the Prophet's wives, and he requested him to place them behind a screen. When the screening order was revealed, 'Umar's view was that they should not go out at all. But this was particularly hard. Therefore, they were permitted to go out for their essential needs.'

Evidence 4: In al-Bukhari's and Muslim's *Ṣaḥīḥ* anthologies, the term *ḥijāb* applies only to the Prophet's wives

A thorough review of the *Ṣaḥīḥ* anthologies of al-Bukhari and Muslim, as well as other hadith anthologies, reveals the word '*ḥijāb*' and corresponding terms, as used in the relevant Qur'anic verse occurs only in relation to the Prophet's wives and to no one else. The Qur'anic verse is concerned with manners to be observed in the Prophet's home, and it says about his wives and the Muslim community: 'When you to ask them for something, do so from behind a screen.' (33: 53) Here are some of the texts of hadiths related by al-Bukhari and Muslim:

ONE: DURING THE PROPHET'S LIFETIME:

- 'Umar said: 'I said: "Messenger of God, good and bad people enter your homes. Perhaps you may wish to order the Mothers of the Believers to be screened." God then revealed the verse giving the screening order.' (Related by al-Bukhari)
- Anas ibn Mālik narrated: 'When God's Messenger married Zaynab bint Jaḥsh, he invited the people. They had their dinner and stayed on chatting. He then did as if he was preparing to go, but they did not rise. When he realized this, he went out. Others left but three people stayed behind. The Prophet came back and wanted to enter, but the people were still sitting. Then they left. I followed and went to the Prophet and told him that they had left. He came back and entered. I wanted to enter behind him, but the screen was dropped between him and myself and God revealed the verse starting: 'Believers, do not enter the Prophet's homes, unless you are given leave...' (33: 53). Muslim adds in his narration: 'Thus the screen became obligatory for the Prophet's wives.' (Related by al-Bukhari and Muslim)
- 'Ā'ishah, the Prophet's wife narrated: '... I went out on an expedition with God's Messenger after the *ḥijāb* was made obligatory... As I was sitting in my place, I was overtaken by sleep. Ṣafwān ibn al-Mu'aṭṭal al-Sulamī al-Dhakwānī was left behind the army. He started moving early at night and reached the place where I was in the morning. He could see the black shape of a sleeping person. He came over to me and recognized me. He used to see me before we were ordered

to be screened. I woke up as he said *innā lillāh wa innā ilayhi rāji'ūn* as he recognized me. I covered my face with my cloak...' (Related by al-Bukhari and Muslim)

- Abu Mūsā al-Ash'arī narrated: '... Umm Salamah called from behind the screen saying to both of them: "Leave some for your mother."' (Related by al-Bukhari and Muslim) Umm Salamah was speaking to Abu Mūsā and Bilāl, referring to herself as their mother because she was the Prophet's wife. The Prophet had given them a jug of water to drink, after he had used it to wash his hands and face. She wanted to have some.
- 'Ā'ishah narrated: 'Sa'd ibn Abi Waqqāṣ and 'Abd ibn Zam'ah were in dispute concerning a young boy. Sa'd said: "Messenger of God, this is my nephew and his father was my brother 'Utbah ibn Abi Waqqāṣ. Look at the similarity between them." 'Abd ibn Zam'ah said: "Messenger of God, this is my brother. He was born in my father's home by his slave woman." The Prophet looked at the boy and he recognized the boy's clear similarity to 'Utbah. He said: "He belongs to you, 'Abd. A child belongs to the bed... Sawdah, let him not see you." Sawdah never saw him.' (Related by al-Bukhari and Muslim) The similarity between the child and 'Utbah was evidence that he was the result of an illegitimate relationship between the slave woman and 'Utbah. Hence the Prophet's ruling that the child belonged to 'Abd as his mother belonged to 'Abd's father, and she gave birth on his bed. The Prophet also ordered Sawdah to screen herself from him because Sawdah was 'Abd's sister. According to the ruling, she would be the child's sister, but because his biological father was a stranger, the Prophet told her not to appear before him.
- 'Ā'ishah narrated: 'My uncle through breastfeeding came over and sought permission to come in. I refused to let him enter until I had asked God's Messenger (peace be upon him)... This took place after we were commanded to remain behind the *ḥijāb*.' (Related by al-Bukhari and Muslim) In a

different report, he said to her: 'Do you screen yourself from me when I am your uncle?' And in Muslim's version: 'He sought permission to enter but she refused him. She told God's Messenger (peace be upon him) and he said to her: 'Do not screen yourself from him.'

- Sa'd ibn Abi Waqqāṣ narrated: "Umar requested permission to enter the Prophet's home. A few Qurashī women were with him, talking to him and asking for more, with their voices louder than his. When 'Umar sought permission, they quickly rose and went behind the screen.' (Related by al-Bukhari and Muslim) Ibn Ḥajar said that the women were some of his wives. However, the hadith does not specify. If they were his wives, then 'asking him for more' means they were requesting more money for family expenses. If they were other women, the hadith refers to their request for more of his explanation of their needs and requests. The Prophet wondered at the speed of their hiding behind the screen when they heard 'Umar's voice, even before the Prophet permitted him to come in. They were in awe of 'Umar.
- 'Ā'ishah narrated: 'When the Prophet heard the news that Ibn Ḥārithah, Ja'far and Ibn Rawāḥah were killed, he sat down looking very sad. I was looking through a narrow door opening.' (Related by al-Bukhari and Muslim) The three were the successive commanders of the Muslim army which fought the Battle of Mu'tah, in which the Muslim army was heavily outnumbered.
- Anas narrated: 'The Prophet did not come out [for the prayer] for three days. The prayer was announced, and Abu Bakr stepped forward. Then the Prophet lifted the screen. When we saw the Prophet's face clear, nothing was to us more delightful. The Prophet signalled to Abu Bakr to step forward [to lead the prayer]. Then the Prophet let down the screen and he was unable to come again before he passed away.' (Related by al-Bukhari and Muslim)

- 'Ā'ishah narrated: 'An effeminate person used to visit the Prophet's wives and they considered him as one who has no desire towards women. The Prophet said: "I think this one knows all there is to know. Do not let him in." Therefore, they did not allow him entry.' (Related by Muslim)
- 'Abd al-Muṭṭallib ibn Rabī'ah ibn al-Ḥārith narrated: '... When God's Messenger finished the Ẓuhr Prayer, we [meaning himself and al-Faḍl ibn 'Abbās] went before him to his apartment, and we stopped there until he came over. He held us by the ear... He remained silent for a long while and we were about to speak to him, but Zaynab signalled to us from behind a screen not to speak...' (Related by Muslim)
- 'Umar ibn al-Khaṭṭāb narrated: 'When the Prophet stayed away from his wives, I came into the mosque and saw people hitting the earth with pebbles. They said that God's Messenger had divorced his wives. This was before they were commanded to be screened...' (The correct thing is that it was after this command was given.) (Related by Muslim)
- 'Ā'ishah narrated that a man came to the Prophet requesting his fatwa. She was listening from behind the door. (Related by Muslim)
- Ibn Mas'ūd narrated: 'God's Messenger (peace be upon him) said to me: "Your permission to come in is that the screen should be lifted."' (Related by Muslim)

Two: During the time of the Prophet's companions:

- Masrūq narrated that he went to 'Ā'ishah and said to her: 'Mother of the Believers, a man sends a sacrifice to the Ka'bah and stays at home. He gives his instructions that his [sacrificial] camel be marked out. Does he remain in consecration, [i.e. *iḥrām*], from that day until the pilgrims are released from consecration?' He said: 'I heard her clapping behind the screen. She said: "I used to prepare the material to mark God's Messenger's sacrifice, and he would send his sacrificial animals to the Ka'bah, but nothing that is lawful for men with their wives becomes unlawful to him at any time until the people returned."' (Related by al-Bukhari and Muslim)

- Speaking about 'Abdullāh ibn al-Zubayr, 'Awf ibn al-Ṭufayl narrated: 'Al-Miswar and 'Abd al-Raḥmān came with him covering him with their upper garments. They sought permission to enter 'Ā'ishah's home. They said: "*Assalāmu 'alaik wa raḥmatullāh.* May we enter?" 'Ā'ishah said: "Come in." They said: "All of us?" She said: "Yes, come in all of you," but she was unaware that Ibn al-Zubayr was with them. When they entered, Ibn al-Zubayr went right in behind the *ḥijāb*.' (Related by al-Bukhari) Ibn al-Zubayr was 'Ā'ishah's nephew as his mother was Asmā', her sister. She had sworn not to speak to him because he said something that angered her. He used this device to meet her and apologize.
- Yūsuf ibn 'Āṣim narrated: 'Marwān was appointed by Mu'āwiyah as Governor of Hijaz. He addressed the people and mentioned Yazīd ibn Mu'āwiyah recommending that he should be chosen to succeed his father. 'Abd al-Raḥmān ibn Abu Bakr said something to him. He said: "Arrest him." He entered 'Ā'ishah's home and they could not get to him. Marwān said: "This is the one regarding whom God revealed the verse that says: 'There is one who says to his parents: Fie on you both! Do you promise me that I shall be resurrected, when generations have passed away before me?'" (46: 17) 'Ā'ishah said from behind her screen: "Nothing of the Qur'an was revealed concerning us [meaning her own family] except that God revealed my innocence."' (Related by al-Bukhari) She was referring to the false accusation levelled at her and that God revealed verses 11-20 of Surah 24, Light, declaring that she was innocent.
- Ibn Jurayj narrated: ''Aṭā' said to us when Ibn Hishām ordered that women must not perform the *ṭawāf* alongside men: "How can he stop them when the Prophet's wives performed the *ṭawāf* alongside men?" I asked him: Was this before or after

the *ḥijāb*? He said: "Yes, indeed. I saw it after the *ḥijab*... I used to go to 'Ā'ishah with 'Ubayd ibn 'Umayr, as she was staying close to Mount Thabīr." I asked: How was she screened? He said: "She was in a small tent with a cover. That was the only thing separating her from us. I saw her wearing a rose-red shirt." (Related by al-Bukhari) In 'Abd al-Razzāq's version: 'She was wearing a saffroned shirt, and I was a young boy.' Thus, he explains why he could see her.

- Sa'd ibn Hishām ibn 'Āmir narrated: '... We went to 'Ā'ishah. We sought permission to enter and she admitted us. When we were in, she asked: 'Is that Ḥakīm?'[4] He said: 'Yes.' She asked: 'Who is with you?' He said: Sa'd ibn Hishām. She asked: 'Which Hishām?' He said: 'Hishām ibn 'Āmir.'[5] She prayed for mercy for him and spoke well of him.' (Related by Muslim)

Evidence 5: Texts confirming that the *ḥijāb* applies only to the Mothers of the Believers, but that are not found in the two *Ṣaḥīḥ* anthologies

The following reports are quoted from Ibn Sa'd's *al-Ṭabaqāt al-Kubrā*:

- 'Abd al-Wāḥid ibn Abi 'Awn al-Dawsī narrated: 'Al-Nu'man ibn Abi al-Jawn al-Kindī travelled to meet God's Messenger as he accepted Islam. He said: "Messenger of God, shall I give you the prettiest woman among the Arabs as a wife? She was married to a cousin of hers who has passed away. She is willing and hopeful that you marry her." God's Messenger married her, at a dowry of twelve *uqiyyahs* and one *nashsh*[6]... God's

4. The Prophet's wives stayed behind a screen when they were visited by any men who were not *maḥram* to them. People frequently went to them asking about the Prophet's guidance in a great variety of matters. They would speak to them, not knowing them. In this case, 'Ā'ishah recognized Ḥakīm by his voice.
5. Hishām was one of the Prophet's companions killed in the Battle of Uhud.
6. The *uqiyyah* is equal to 40 dirhams and the *nashsh* is half of that. This made her dowry 500 dirhams.

Messenger sent Abu Usayd al-Sāʿidī with him. When they went to her in her home and she admitted him, Abu Usayd said: "No man ever sees any of the Prophet's wives." This was after the *ḥijāb* obligation. She sent to him requesting him to release her. He said: "You shall have a screen separating you from any man you are speaking to, except your immediate relatives whom you cannot marry."

- Abu Usayd al-Sāʿidī said to a woman from al-Jawn clan whom the Prophet returned to her people before the consummation of their marriage: 'Stay in your home and remain behind a screen from all men other than your *maḥrams*. No one may aspire to marry you after God's Messenger, as you are one of the Mothers of the Believers.' She stayed at home, with none hoping to marry her. No one could see her except her *maḥrams*, until she passed away during 'Uthmān's reign. She was at her people's home in Najd.
- Ibn 'Abbās narrated: 'Al-Muhājir ibn Abi Umayyah ibn al-Mughīrah married Asmā' bint al-Nuʿmān after the Prophet. 'Umar wanted to punish them both. She said: "By God, he did not screen me and I was never called Mother of the Believers." 'Umar never did that.'
- Dāwūd ibn Abi Hind narrated that when the Prophet passed away, he was married to a woman from Kindah called Qatīlah. She joined her people when they became apostates. Sometime later, 'Ikrimah ibn Abi Jahl married her. Abu Bakr was extremely sad when this happened. 'Umar said to him: 'By God, she was not his wife. He neither offered her the choice [he offered to his wives] nor did he screen her.' Both al-Ṭabarī and Ibn Kathīr mention in their commentaries on the Qur'an the same case somewhat differently, naming the woman as Qatīlah bint al-Ashʿath. There is no mention of apostasy in this version. It adds that Abu Bakr was reassured by 'Umar's words.

Evidence 6: The Prophet's wives were denied permission to join jihad after the *ḥijāb* obligation, but other women were permitted

> Note: We have made sure that all the cases mentioned, up to and including Evidence 11, took place after the verse ordering the Prophet's wives to be screened was revealed.

The Prophet's wives were given permission to take part in jihad before they were ordered to be screened. Anas narrated: 'During the Battle of Uhud people deserted the Prophet (peace be upon him)... I saw 'Ā'ishah bint Abu Bakr and Umm Sulaym. Both lifted their skirts and I could see their anklets. They quickly jerked waterskins on their backs and poured the water in people's mouths, then returned fast to fill them again and moved forward to pour it in people's mouths.' (Related by al-Bukhari and Muslim)

Yet the Prophet's wives were denied permission to take part in jihad after the *ḥijāb* order was revealed. 'Ā'ishah reports that she said to the Prophet: 'We have learnt that jihad is the best type of deed. Should we not take part in jihad?' He said: 'For you, the best type of jihad is a properly conducted pilgrimage.' Another version of this hadith quotes her saying: 'I requested the Prophet's permission to go on jihad, but he said: "Your jihad is the hajj."' (Related by al-Bukhari)

'Ā'ishah also narrated: 'The Prophet's wives asked him about jihad, and he said: "Fine jihad is the hajj."' (Related by al-Bukhari)

Yet the Prophet's wives joined him on some military expeditions, but this was for companionship, not to participate in jihad. 'Ā'ishah, the Prophet's wife, narrated: '... God's Messenger (peace be upon him) drew lots between us as he was about to travel. Whoever was drawn out would be in his company. Once as he was going on a military expedition, he drew lots between us and it came out in my favour. I went with God's Messenger (peace be upon him) after the screening was made obligatory. I was carried and put down in my howdah...' (Related by al-Bukhari and Muslim)

'Ā'ishah narrated: 'When the Prophet intended to travel, he drew lots between his wives. On one occasion, the draw came out in favour of 'Ā'ishah and Ḥafṣah. When it was night, the Prophet would march alongside 'Ā'ishah and conversed [with her]. Ḥafṣah said [to 'Ā'ishah]: "Would you like to ride my camel tonight and I ride yours: you will be looking at [different] things and I will?" She said: "Yes." I rode...' (Related by al-Bukhari and Muslim)

Al-Miswar ibn Makhramah and Marwān narrated, each confirming the other's narration. They said: 'God's Messenger set out at the time of al-Hudaybiyah... Suhayl ibn 'Amr came over. He said: "Let us write down an agreement between you and us." The Prophet called in the scribe and said: "Write down"... When the matter of the written agreement was over, the Prophet said to his Companions: "Get up and slaughter your sacrifice. When you have finished, shave your heads." By God, not a single person among them got up, even when he repeated this three times. When none of them did, he went in to Umm Salamah and he mentioned to her what he suffered...' (Related by al-Bukhari)

'Ā'ishah, the Prophet's wife, said: 'We set out with God's Messenger (peace be upon him) on a journey, and when we were at al-Baydā' [a desert area close to Madinah], or at Dhāt al-Jaysh, a necklace of mine was dropped. The Prophet stayed on while it was being looked for. The people stayed on with him but they had no water. People spoke to Abu Bakr and said: "Do you realise what 'Ā'ishah has done? She has caused God's Messenger and the people to stay on with no water around, and they have no water." Abu Bakr came over to me while God's Messenger had placed his head on my thigh and slept.

He said: "You have stopped God's Messenger when the people are near no water spring and they have no water." 'Ā'ishah said: Abu Bakr remonstrated with me...' (Related by al-Bukhari and Muslim)

However, a number of Muslim women took part in jihad after the *ḥijāb* was made obligatory. Anas narrated: 'God's Messenger (peace be upon him) set out on a military expedition to Khaybar. We prayed Fajr close to it, when it was still dark... When we entered its outskirts, the Prophet said: "*Allah-u akbar.* When we strike in their midst, terrible will be the morning of those who were already warned." He repeated this three times... We took it over after a hard battle. The captives were assembled. Diḥyah came over and said: "Prophet, give me a maid from the captives." He said: "Go and choose one"... He took Ṣafiyyah bint Ḥuyay. A man came to the Prophet and said: "Prophet of God, you have given Ṣafiyyah bint Ḥuyay, the mistress of Qurayẓah and al-Naḍīr, to Diḥyah. She is good for none other than you." The Prophet said: "Call him to bring her." When he brought her, the Prophet looked at her. He said to him: "Choose a different captive"." The Prophet set her free and married her... When he was on the way back, Umm Sulaym prepared her for him.' (Related by al-Bukhari and Muslim)

Anas narrated that Umm Sulaym had a dagger on the day of the Battle of Ḥunayn. Abu Ṭalḥah [her husband] saw her, and he said: 'Messenger of God, here is Umm Sulaym and she has a dagger.' The Prophet asked her what the dagger was for, and she replied: 'I am arming myself with it so that if an unbeliever comes close to me, I will stab him in his belly.' The Prophet laughed. (Related by Muslim)

Anas ibn Mālik reports: 'The Prophet visited [Umm Ḥarām] bint Milḥān... He slept [at her place] and when he woke up, he smiled. She asked him what caused him to smile. He said: "I was shown a group of my followers going for jihad, riding into the blue sea, looking like kings on their thrones..." She said: "Messenger of God! Pray to

God to make me one of them." He said: "My Lord, make her one of them"... She went on the maritime expedition during the reign of Mu'āwiyah ibn Abi Sufyān, accompanied by Bint Quraẓah, and when she disembarked, she fell off her mount and died.' (Related by al-Bukhari and Muslim)

Yazīd ibn Hurmuz narrated that Najdah wrote to Ibn 'Abbās asking him about five things... In his response, Ibn 'Abbas wrote: 'You asked me whether God's Messenger took women with him on his military expeditions? Yes, he used to take women and they treated the wounded and were given gifts from the war gains.' (Related by Muslim)

It should be noted that the Battle of Khaybar took place in the first month of year 7 AH, while the Battle of Ḥunayn was in Shawwāl of year 8 AH, i.e. both were after the *ḥijāb* obligation was ordered. Umm Ḥarām's participation in the maritime expedition was many years after the Prophet had passed away. The hadith mentioning Ibn 'Abbās's correspondence says that the Prophet 'used to take women...' which suggests that this continued and was not confined to any particular period. There are many instances of the participation of Muslim women in jihad after the *ḥijāb* obligation. For further details, reference may be made to Chapter 4 of Volume 2 of this series.

Evidence 7: Unlike other Muslim women, the Prophet's wives perform the hajj without mixing with men

- Ibrahīm ibn 'Abd al-Raḥmān ibn 'Awf narrated: 'At the time of his last performance of the hajj, 'Umar permitted the Prophet's wives to perform the hajj. He sent with them 'Uthmān ibn 'Affān and 'Abd al-Raḥmān.' (Related by al-Bukhari)

Imam Ibn Ḥajar said: 'Al-Bukhari relates this hadith in this short way... ʿAbdān adds in the version narrated by al-Bayhaqī: "ʿUthmān used to call out that no one was permitted to come near them or see them. They rode in their howdahs carried by camels. When they stopped, he would ensure that they stopped at the top of the passage, so that no one was allowed to reach them, while ʿAbd al-Raḥmān and ʿUthmān stopped at the bottom." In another report stated by Ibn Saʿd: "ʿUthmān travelled ahead of them and ʿAbd al-Raḥmān behind them." In another report stated by Ibn Saʿd with a sound chain of transmission that includes Abu Isḥāq al-Sabīʿī, he says: "I saw the Prophet's wives screened in their howdahs that were well covered, during the reign of al-Mughīrah ibn Shuʿbah." It is clear that he meant when al-Mughīrah was Governor of Kufah during Muʿāwiyah's reign as Caliph.' This addition quoted from al-Bayhaqī by Ibn Ḥajar is narrated by Ibn Saʿd with a sound chain of transmission.

- Ibn Jurayj narrated: "ʿAṭā' said to us when Ibn Hishām ordered that women must not perform the *ṭawāf* alongside men: "How can he stop them when the Prophet's wives performed the *ṭawāf* alongside men?" I asked him: Was this before or after the *ḥijāb*? He said: "Yes, indeed. I saw it after the *ḥijāb*." I said: How could they mix with men? He said: "They did not mix with them. ʿĀ'ishah used to perform the *ṭawāf* and she was well-separated from men. One woman said to her: 'Come over so that we kiss [the Black Stone].' ʿĀ'ishah said: 'You may go,' but she herself refused. The Prophet's wives used to come out at night, well disguised, and perform the *ṭawāf* alongside men, but when they entered the Grand Mosque, they stopped until they could enter, while the men were ordered to leave."' (Related by al-Bukhari) (Note: this is a bit confusing: hence the underlining rather than a lengthy note.)
- Umm al-Ḥuṣayn: 'I went out with the Prophet on his Farewell Pilgrimage. I saw him when he did the stoning at Jamrat

al-'Aqabah and then left. He was on his camel, and Bilāl and Usāmah were with him. One of them was leading his camel and the other holding his robe above the Prophet's head to shelter him from the sun. The Prophet said many things, before I heard him saying: "If a slave whose ears and nose have been cut (and the reporter thought that she described the slave as 'black') is appointed your leader and he implements God's Book, then you must listen and obey him."' (Related by Muslim)

- 'Abdullāh ibn 'Abbās narrated: 'On the Day of Sacrifice, the Prophet (peace be upon him) took al-Faḍl ibn 'Abbās behind him on the back of his she-camel... The Prophet stopped to answer people's questions. A pretty woman from Khath'am came to the Prophet to ask him for a ruling... She said: "Messenger of God, the obligation to perform the hajj came at a time when my father is an elderly man who cannot sit up on his camel. Is it sufficient for him that I perform the pilgrimage on his behalf?" The Prophet said: "Yes."' (Related by al-Bukhari and Muslim)
- Ibn 'Abbās narrated that the Prophet met a group of travellers at al-Rawḥā' and asked them who they were. They said: 'We are Muslims. Who are you?' He said: 'I am God's Messenger.' A woman lifted her baby son and asked him: 'Can this one perform the hajj?' He said: 'Yes, and you earn a reward.' (Related by Muslim)

All these hadiths confirm that the way the Prophet's wives performed the hajj was different because they were the only ones under the *ḥijāb* obligation. Therefore, they had to be screened from men as far as that was possible. They performed the *ṭawāf* at night under disguise, and away from men, while other Muslim women performed the *ṭawāf* at all times of the day and night, kissing the Black Stone if they could manage to do so, mixing with men during the performance of the hajj rituals. It should be remembered that the Prophet offered his pilgrimage in year 10 AH.

Evidence 8: The *ḥijāb* applied to the Prophet's wives but not to his slave women

ଓ Anas narrated: 'The Prophet stopped three days between Khaybar and Madinah so as to have his wedding with Ṣafiyyah bint Ḥuyay. I invited Muslims to attend the bridal dinner which contained neither bread nor meat. He ordered hides to be spread and dates, dried milk and ghee were placed on them. This was the dinner he served. [In reference to Ṣafiyyah] some Muslims said: "She is either one of the Mothers of the Believers, or she is one his right hand possesses [i.e. a slave]." Then they said: "If he screens her, she is a Mother of the Believers, but if he does not, she is one he possesses." When he was about to leave, he prepared her place behind him [on his mount] and put a screen between her and the people.' (Related by al-Bukhari and Muslim)

The hadith implies that the Prophet's Companions were certain that the *ḥijāb* applied only to the Prophet's wives and to no other woman; not even to his slave women, even though they were pretty. The distinction here is not between free women and slave women. If slave women are pretty, then it is better that they should be as well covered as free women. This is stated by Ibn Taymiyyah in a long discourse which may be summed up as follows: 'It is more logical and reasonable that at least some slave women should be excepted, because they are more likely to stir temptation and desire as they did not need to cover themselves fully, but could show their charms and adornments.' This was even more so, if slave women were chosen as bed fellows, as Ibn al-Qayyim says. All this proves that the distinction here is that of the Mothers of Believers who are distinguished from all women, whether free or slave.

Evidence 9: The *ḥijāb* applied to the Prophet's wives, but not to his daughters

God says in the Qur'an: 'The case of Jesus in the sight of God is the same as the case of Adam. He created him of dust and then said to him: "Be," and he was. This is the truth from your Lord: be not, then, among the doubters. If anyone should dispute with you about this [truth] after all the knowledge you have received, say: Come. Let us summon our sons and your sons, our women and your women, and ourselves and yourselves; then let us pray humbly and solemnly and invoke God's curse upon the ones who are telling a lie.' (3: 59-61)

Ibn Kathīr wrote in his commentary on these verses: '"Let us summon our sons and your sons, our women and your women..." This means that we bring them to be present at the time of mutual supplication... The following morning the Prophet came to the appointment, bringing with him his daughter Fāṭimah and her two young sons al-Ḥasan and al-Ḥusayn. At the time, he had several wives.'

Another report says: '... Al-'Āqib and al-Ṭayyib, chiefs of the Najran delegation, came to see the Prophet. He invited them to join him in mutual supplication "that God's curse befalls those who are liars". They agreed with him that they should do this the following day. The next morning, the Prophet came, holding the hands of 'Alī, Fāṭimah, al-Ḥasan and al-Ḥusayn. He sent to them to come over, but they refused... Jābir said: 'It was concerning them that this verse was revealed: "If anyone should dispute with you about this [truth] after all the knowledge you have received, say: Come. Let us summon our sons and your sons, our women and your women, and ourselves and yourselves; then let us pray humbly and solemnly and invoke God's curse upon the ones who are telling a lie." (3: 61) "Ourselves and yourselves" these are God's Messenger and 'Alī ibn Abi Ṭālib; "our sons" these are al-Ḥasan and al-Ḥusayn; "our women" this refers to Fāṭimah.' The hadith is narrated in this way by al-Ḥākim in his *al-Mustadrak*, narrated by ʿAlī ibn ʿĪsā. Al-Ḥākim comments: 'This is an authentic hadith according to Muslim's conditions but neither al-Bukhari nor Muslim relates it. This is what he said. However, Abu Dāwūd al-Ṭayālisī relates it with a chain of transmission from Shuʿbah, from al-Mughīrah, from al-Shaʿbī, as a *mursal*, i.e. incomplete chain. This is more accurate. Similar reports quote Ibn ʿAbbās and al-Barā'.'

The Qur'anic verse and its explanation make clear that the *ḥijāb* was not obligatory for Fāṭimah. This is why she went with the Prophet to take part in the mutual supplication, but none of the Prophet's wives joined him. The narrator says that the Prophet 'had several wives at the time'. This means that the only woman to attend was Fāṭimah, although the Prophet had several wives. In my view, the only reason for their absence is that they were ordered to remain behind a screen.

- Anas narrated: 'When the Prophet's illness aggravated, he kept losing consciousness. Fāṭimah said: "How distressed my father is." He said: "Your father shall not be in distress after today." When he passed away, she said: "O my father! He answered his Lord's call. O my father! The garden of Paradise is his place of dwelling. O my father! To Gabriel we announce his death"... When he was buried, Fāṭimah said: "Anas, were you pleased as you hurled dust over God's Messenger's body?"' (Related by al-Bukhari)
- ʿĀ'ishah narrated: 'Fāṭimah and al-ʿAbbās went to Abu Bakr requesting their inheritance from God's Messenger. They were requesting their land in Fadak and their shares in Khaybar. Abu Bakr said to them: "I heard God's Messenger (peace be upon him) say: 'We [prophets] do not bequeath inheritance. Whatever we leave behind is given to charity [i.e. *ṣadaqah*]. Members of Muhammad's household take their need from this money." Abu Bakr added: "By God, whatever

I saw the Prophet using this income for, I will do the same." Fāṭimah boycotted him, and she did not speak to him until she died.' In a different version: 'She boycotted Abu Bakr and continued to do so until she died.' (Related by al-Bukhari and Muslim)

Imam Ibn Ḥajar argued that some scholars said that her boycott was merely an avoidance of meeting him. This is not the same as a forbidden boycott. This forbidden type involves that they meet and each of them turns away from the other. It appears that when Fāṭimah left Abu Bakr in anger, she was preoccupied with her sorrow and then with her illness. Although Abu Bakr cited the quoted hadith, she was angry because she understood the hadith differently from Abu Bakr's understanding. It appears that she felt that the general statement 'we do not bequeath inheritance' had a specific significance. According to this understanding, the revenue of the land and real property he left behind could be inherited. On the other hand, Abu Bakr upheld the general meaning of the statement. Thus, they differed on a point which admitted different ways of understanding. When he insisted on his view, she refrained from meeting him.

Al-Bayhaqī narrated through al-Sha'bī that 'Abu Bakr visited Fāṭimah during her illness. 'Alī said to her: "Here is Abu Bakr seeking permission to visit you." She said: "Do you like that I admit him?" He said: "Yes." Abu Bakr entered and sought reconciliation with her until she was pleased with him.' Although this report is of the *mursal* type, its chain of transmission up to al-Sha'bī is authentic. On the basis of this narration, the question of whether Fāṭimah's long boycott of Abu Bakr was permissible or not does not arise. If al-Sha'bī's narration is confirmed, the problem is sorted out. It is more likely that it is so, because Fāṭimah was very wise and devout.

We can reconcile the texts of al-Bukhari and Muslim on the one hand and al-Sha'bī's narration on the other. His narration makes clear that it was Abu Bakr who went to visit her during her final illness. Thus, the statement that she continued her boycott until she died would mean that she did not go to him. The other statement, 'she did not speak to him until she died' would mean that she did not speak to him about the inheritance until she was close to death.

At this point we would like to draw attention to the Qur'anic verse that says: 'God only wants to remove all that is loathsome from you, you members of the [Prophet's] household, and to purify you fully.' (33: 33) We further quote the hadith narrated by 'Ā'ishah: 'The Prophet came out in the morning, wearing an untailored cloak made of black hair and showing drawings of a camel's saddle.[7] Al-Ḥasan came over and he took him in, then al-Ḥusayn came over and he took him in. Fāṭimah then came and he took her in, and then 'Alī came over and he took him in. He then said: "God only wants to remove all that is loathsome from you, you members of the [Prophet's] household, and to purify you fully."' (Related by Muslim)

In this hadith, the Prophet extends honour to his daughter Fāṭimah, her husband and her two sons, including them in the meaning of the verse that is addressed to his wives (may God be pleased with all of them). We may reflect on this purity God has bestowed on Fāṭimah, and how she attained a sublime status of honour as mentioned in the following hadith: 'The best women of heaven are Khadījah bint Khuwaylid, Fāṭimah bint Muhammad, Mary bint 'Imrān and Asiyah bint Muzāḥim, Pharaoh's wife.' All this purity and honour, yet there was no need to make the *ḥijāb* obligatory on her. This confirms that the *ḥijāb* was made obligatory for the Prophet's wives for something that applied to them alone and to no other Muslim woman. The relevant Qur'anic verse says: 'When you ask the Prophet's wives for something, do so from behind a screen: this makes for greater purity

7. It was a normal way of decorating clothes and curtains with drawings of saddles and similar objects.

for your hearts and theirs.' (33: 53) Most likely, the purity this verse speaks of relates to what comes next of forbidding them to marry anyone after the Prophet: 'Moreover, it does not behove you to give offence to God's Messenger, just as it would not behove you ever to marry his widows after he has passed away. That is certainly an enormity in God's sight.' (33: 53) Undoubtedly, the way the verse is phrased suggests this. We will speak about this point in more detail at the end of this theme.

Evidence 10: Noble female Companions of the Prophet met men without the *ḥijāb*

Umm al-Faḍl bint al-Ḥārith: She was married to al-ʿAbbās ibn ʿAbd al-Muṭṭalib, the Prophet's uncle. The Prophet said: 'The four sisters are believers: Maymūnah, Umm al-Faḍl, Salmā, and Asmā' bint ʿUmays: [Asmā'] is their sister through having the same mother.' Umm al-Faḍl narrated: 'On the Day of Arafat, some people at my place disputed whether the Prophet was fasting or not. Some said that he was fasting and others claimed that he was not. I sent him a cup of milk, as he was on his camel, and he drank it.' (Related by al-Bukhari and Muslim)

Imam Ibn Ḥajar said: 'This hadith includes several important points, one of which is the permissibility of scholarly discussion between men and women.'

Asmā' bint ʿUmays: She was married to Jaʿfar ibn Abi Ṭālib, and the Prophet said of her that she was one of the four sisters who were believers. He said to her husband: 'You are like me in looks and manners.'

Abu Mūsā narrated: 'We heard of the Prophet's migration to Madinah when we were in Yemen. We left to join him, and I was with two of my brothers: one was Abu Burdah and the other Abu

Ruhm, and I was the youngest. We were 53 or 52 people of our tribe. We took a boat, but our boat landed us at Negus's land in Abyssinia where we met Ja'far ibn Abi Ṭālib and we stayed with him until we all came together to Madinah. We met the Prophet when he had taken Khaybar. Some people used to say to us, the people who came on the boat: 'We migrated before you.' Asmā' bint 'Umays, who came with us, visited Ḥafṣah, the Prophet's wife. She was one of those who migrated to Abyssinia along with others. 'Umar came in while Asmā' was there. When he saw Asmā', 'Umar asked [his daughter]: 'Who is this?' She said: 'Asmā' bint 'Umays.' 'Umar said: 'The Abyssinian one? The seafarer one?' Asmā' said: 'Yes.' He said: 'We migrated ahead of you. Therefore, we have more claim to God's Messenger than you.'

Feeling angry, she said: 'No way. By God, you were with God's Messenger and he fed the hungry ones and admonished the ones who were ignorant. We were in Abyssinia, the land of alien, hateful people, enduring that for the sake of God and His Messenger. By God, I shall taste neither food nor drink until I have mentioned what you said to God's Messenger (peace be upon him). We were hurt and scared, and I shall mention this to the Prophet and ask him. By God, I shall neither lie nor twist. I shall say no more than what has been said.'

When the Prophet came in, she [Asmā' bint 'Umays] said: 'God's Messenger! 'Umar has just said so-and-so.' The Prophet asked her, 'What was your reply to him?' She said: 'I said such-and-such.' The Prophet said: 'He does not have a better claim to me than you. He and his fellow Muslims have the reward of one migration, while you, the people of the boat, shall have the reward of two migrations.' Asmā' added: 'Abu Mūsā and the people who came on the boat from Abyssinia came in groups to see me asking about this hadith. Nothing in this world gave them more joy and greater happiness than what God's Messenger said about them.'" Abu Burdah said that Asmā' said: 'Abu Mūsā came over requesting that I narrate the hadith to him again.' (Related by al-Bukhari and Muslim)

When Ja'far, her husband, died, Asmā' bint 'Umays married Abu Bakr of whom the Prophet said: 'The one who did me the greatest favour in his friendship and money is Abu Bakr. Were I to take an intimate friend other than my Lord, I would have chosen Abu Bakr. However, the brotherhood and intimacy of Islam is sufficient.' (Related by al-Bukhari and Muslim)

'Abdullāh ibn 'Amr ibn al-'Āṣ narrated: 'Some people from the Hāshim clan visited Asmā' bint 'Umays when she was married to Abu Bakr al-Ṣiddīq. Abu Bakr came in and saw them, and he disliked this. He mentioned this to the Prophet and said: "I saw nothing but good." God's Messenger said: "God has made her innocent of anything untoward." Then the Prophet stood on the platform and said: "After this day of mine, let no man enter the place of any woman whose husband is absent unless accompanied by one or two men."' (Related by Muslim)

It appears that the Prophet wanted to say that when a group of men visit a woman this dispels any suspicion. This reassured Abu Bakr, as those who were with Asmā' were a group of people. Al-Ṭabarānī narrated from Qays ibn Abi Ḥāzim: 'We visited Abu Bakr during his illness. I saw a white woman, with henna on her hands, keeping flies away from him. She was Asmā' bint 'Umays.'

Asmā' was later married to 'Alī ibn Abi Ṭālib of whom the Prophet said at the time of the Battle of Khaybar: 'I shall give the banner tomorrow to a man whom God and His Messenger love.' (Related by al-Bukhari and Muslim)

Tamīm ibn Abi Salamah narrated that "'Amr ibn al-'Ās went to 'Alī ibn Abi Ṭālib's home seeking something. 'Alī was not at home, and he left. He returned later twice or three times. 'Alī came afterwards and said: "Could you not have entered when your need is with her?" 'Amr said: "We have been forbidden to enter their [i.e. women's] places unless permitted by their husbands."'

Asmā' bint Abu Bakr: She was married to al-Zubayr ibn al-'Awwām of whom the Prophet said: 'Every prophet had a true supporter and my one is al-Zubayr.' (Related by al-Bukhari and Muslim)

Asmā' reports: 'I went to see 'Ā'ishah, but I found her praying. I asked: "What is the matter with people?" She pointed to the sky,[8] and I saw that the people were standing up in prayer. She said: "*Subḥān Allah*, which means, limitless is God in His glory," I asked: "Is this a sign from God?" She affirmed this with a head signal. I joined the prayer and stood there until I almost fainted. There was close to me a waterskin and I opened it pouring water on my head. God's Messenger finished the prayer when the sun had become clear. He addressed the people, praising God as He deserves to be praised. He then said: 'Meanwhile'.... Some Anṣārī women were talking together, and I went towards them to silence them....'" In another version: 'The Prophet addressed the people and he mentioned the test in the grave when a person is examined. When he mentioned this, Muslims gave a cry of fear.' (Related by al-Bukhari)

Imam Ibn Ḥajar said that al-Bukhari related this hadith of Asmā' bint Abu Bakr in a much shorter version. Both al-Nasā'ī and al-Ismā'īlī relate it through the same chain of transmission as al-Bukhari, adding the following: 'When he mentioned this, Muslims gave a cry of fear which prevented my understanding of the last thing God's Messenger (peace be upon him) said. When they calmed down, I said to a man who was close to me: "May God bless you! What did God's Messenger say at the end of his speech?" He told me that the Prophet said: "It was revealed to me that you shall have a trial in your graves which is nearly as hard as the trial of the Impostor."'

8. This was an occasion of a solar eclipse. At that time, the Prophet called on the Muslim community to come to the mosque and he led them in a special, and very long prayer. Asmā' was unaware of this when she went to her sister. Hence, her questions. Her question about a sign from God refers to the eclipse.

Abu Nawfal narrated: 'Al-Ḥajjāj then sent to Asmā' bint Abu Bakr asking her to come to him. She refused. He sent his messenger again with the message, "You shall come to me or I will send someone to drag you here by your hair." She again refused, telling the messenger to tell him: "By God, I shall not come to you even though you send someone to drag me by my hair." When he was told this, he said: "Give me my shoes." He went out feeling triumphant. When he arrived at her place, he asked her: "What do you think of what I did with God's enemy?" She said: "You have ruined this present life for him while he ruined your future life for you. I am told that you refer to him as the son of the woman with two girdles. I am that woman. I used one to tie up the food for the Prophet and Abu Bakr and cover it, and the other was the one no woman can do without. God's Messenger told us that from the tribe of Thaqīf, there will come a liar and a destroyer. We have certainly seen the liar.[9] As for the destroyer, I feel that you are the one." He left her without saying a word.' (Related by Muslim)

Umm Sulaym al-Ghumaysā' bint Milḥān: God's Messenger said: 'I entered heaven and I heard someone walking. I asked who was walking. They said: This is al-Ghumayṣā' bint Milḥān.' (Related by Muslim) She was married to Abu Ṭalḥah al-Anṣārī of whom Anas [Umm Sulaym's son] said: 'During the Battle of Uḥud, people dispersed away from the Prophet, but Abu Ṭalḥah was protecting him with his shield. The Prophet rose up to look at the people.

9. Asma' was able to put things in the proper perspective. When al-Ḥajjāj referred to her son as 'God's enemy' she told him that by killing her son, he spoilt his life on earth, while he was yet to account to God for killing him. The point she mentions about her girdles refers to the time when the Prophet and her father, Abu Bakr, migrated to Madinah. She went to their hiding place to take food for them. On the day they were to start their journey, she forgot to wrap the food up, so she tore her girdle in two, using one part to wrap the food and the other to hold her clothes up. The reference to the liar from the Thaqīf tribe points to al-Mukhtār ibn 'Ubaydillāh who claimed himself a prophet. Al-Ḥajjāj belonged to the same tribe.

Abu Ṭalḥah said to him: "May my parents be sacrificed for you, Messenger of God. Do not rise, lest an arrow of theirs may hit you. I lay my life down for you".' (Related by al-Bukhari and Muslim)

Anas ibn Mālik narrated: 'God's Messenger (peace be upon him) used to take Umm Sulaym and some women from the Anṣār on his military expeditions. They would provide [the fighters] with drinking water and treat the wounded.' (Related by Muslim)

Anas narrated: '... When God's Messenger was on the way [meaning on the way back from Khaybar to Madinah] Umm Sulaym prepared her [meaning Ṣafiyyah bint Ḥuyay] and took her to him at nightfall.' (Related by al-Bukhari and Muslim)

Umm Ayman: The woman who nursed God's Messenger when he was a child. He married her to Zayd ibn Ḥārithah and she gave him his son Usāmah ibn Zayd.

Anas narrated: 'Abu Bakr said to 'Umar after the Prophet had passed away: "Let us go and visit Umm Ayman as God's Messenger used to visit her." When they were with her she wept. They said: "Why do you cry? What God gives His Messenger is better for him." She said: "What makes me cry is not that I am not unaware that being with God is better for His Messenger. I am weeping because divine revelations have ceased." She thus stirred their tears and they wept with her.' (Related by Muslim)

Faṭīmah bint Qays and Umm Sharīk: Fāṭimah was one of the early migrants. It is narrated that she said: 'When I became without a husband [i.e. after her divorce] 'Abd al-Raḥmān ibn 'Awf and other Companions of the Prophet proposed to me. The Prophet wanted me to marry his *mawlā*, Usāmah ibn Zayd. I was told that the Prophet had said: "Whoever loves me should love Usāmah." Therefore, when God's Messenger (peace be upon him) spoke to me, I said: "I place myself in your hand. Marry me to whomever you wish..." I married him and God has honoured me by [marrying] Ibn Zayd; and God has been kind to me by [marrying] Ibn Zayd... God made this marriage good and I was happy with him.'

'Ubaydullāh ibn 'Abdullāh ibn 'Utbah reported that Abu 'Amr ibn Ḥafṣ ibn al-Mughīrah set out with 'Alī ibn Abi Ṭālib, going to Yemen. He sent to his wife Fāṭimah bint Qays that he had divorced her the last of three times. Al-Ḥārith ibn Hishām and 'Ayyāsh ibn Abi Rabī'ah sent her some maintenance and said to her: 'By God, you are not entitled to any maintenance unless you are pregnant.' She came to the Prophet and told him what they said. He said: 'He does not owe you maintenance.' She asked him permission to move and he permitted her....

In another version, the Prophet told her to stay with Umm Sharīk [during her waiting period]. Umm Sharīk was a wealthy woman from the Anṣār and she spent much for God's sake. She welcomed many guests. Fāṭimah reports that she told the Prophet: 'I will do that.' He then told her: 'No, do not move there. Umm Sharīk is frequently visited by guests. I dislike that your head cover may drop or your robe may be lifted and expose your legs, which lets people see of you what you dislike to be seen. Move instead to your cousin Ibn Umm Maktūm's home.' She moved there. (Related by Muslim) Ibn Umm Maktūm was a blind man from the Fihr clan of the Quraysh. She belonged to the same branch of the clan.

Al-Sha'bī narrated: 'We visited Fāṭimah bint Qays and she served us dates of the Ibn Ṭāb variety and the Sult drink. I asked her about a three-time divorced woman: where does she observe her waiting period. She said: "My husband divorced me three times. The Prophet (peace be upon him) permitted me to observe my waiting period at my own people's home."' (Related by Muslim)

Umm Ḥarām bint Milḥān: She was the wife of ʿUbādah ibn al-Ṣāmit. ʿUbādah attended the ʿAqabah pledge given by 70 people from the Anṣār and was one of the 12 *naqībs* or supervisors. He took part in the Battles of Badr, Uḥud, the Moat and all military confrontations with God's Messenger (peace be upon him).

ʿUmayr ibn al-Aswad al-ʿAnsī narrated that he visited ʿUbādah ibn al-Ṣāmit when he was living in a house at Homs, and Umm Ḥarām was with him. ʿUmayr said: 'Umm Ḥarām narrated to us that she heard God's Messenger (peace be upon him) say: "The first army of my community to undertake jihad through the sea have earned it."[10] Umm Ḥarām said: "Messenger of God, am I one of them?" He said: "You are one of them." He then said: "The first army of my community to attack the capital of the Byzantine Emperor are forgiven their sins." I said: "Messenger of God, am I one of them?" He said: "No."' (Related by al-Bukhari)

We mentioned Umm Ḥarām earlier, under Evidence 6. She was Umm Sulaym's sister.

Subayʿah bint al-Ḥārith al-Aslamiyyah: One of the migrants who gave their pledges of allegiance to God's Messenger. She was married to Saʿd ibn Khawlah of the Muhājirīn. He took part in the battles of Badr, Uḥud, the Moat and also al-Hudaybiyah.

Subayʿah bint al-Ḥārith was married to Saʿd ibn Khawlah, but he died during the Farewell Pilgrimage. Only a short while after that she gave birth to her child. When she regained her strength, she started to wear make-up expecting a proposal. Abu al-Sanʿbil ibn Baʿkak came to her and said: "How come you are adorned expecting a proposal, hoping to get married? By God, you cannot get married

10. The expression 'have earned it' means that they have done something which ensures their admittance into heaven.

before the lapse of four months and ten days [after your husband's death]." Subay'ah said: "When he said this to me, I put on my clothes in the evening and went to God's Messenger (peace be upon him) and I asked him about this. He told me that I had finished my waiting period when I gave birth and he left it up to me to get married if I wished." (Related by al-Bukhari and Muslim)

Su'ayrah al-Asadiyyah (Umm Zufar): 'Aṭā' ibn Rabāḥ narrated: 'Ibn 'Abbās asked me: "Would you like me to show you a woman who will definitely be in heaven?" I said: "Yes, indeed." Ibn 'Abbās said: "It is this black woman. She came to the Prophet and said: 'I suffer from epilepsy and I may be exposed when I have a fit. Pray for me.' The Prophet said to her: 'If you wish you bear your affliction with patience and you will be in heaven, or I will pray to God for you to be cured.' She said: 'I will bear it with patience, but pray for me that I may not be exposed during a fit.' He prayed for her."' (Related by al-Bukhari and Muslim)

Evidence 11: The Prophet and his Companions met women without a screen

In obligatory prayers

Fāṭimah bint Qays reports: '... After I had finished my waiting period, I heard the Prophet's caller announcing, "All come to prayer,"[11] and I went to the mosque and offered the prayer with the Prophet. I was in the women's row that was immediately to the men's back.' In another version: 'The call went out to come to prayer, and I moved forward with other people: I was in the first women's row which was just next to the last of the men's rows.' (Related by Muslim)

11. This was how public meetings were announced. The caller would go around making this call and the people would then flock to the mosque where there would be a short prayer before the Prophet made whatever announcement he wanted to make.

In the Eid Prayer

Umm 'Aṭiyyah narrated: 'We were ordered to come over on the Eid day, and even bring virgin women to the prayer place and bring out the women having their period. They would be behind the people, glorifying God as the [worshippers] did and join them in supplication, hoping to earn the blessings and purity of the day.' (Related by al-Bukhari and Muslim)

In the prayer at the time of eclipse

'Ā'ishah, the Prophet's wife, narrated: '... God's Messenger (peace be upon him) rode one morning, but the sun eclipsed. He came back in mid-morning, passing by his apartments. (In a version related by Muslim: I went out with some women close to the apartments in the mosque.) He stood up praying and the people joined him. That was a very long prayer...' (Related by al-Bukhari and Muslim)

In al-Bukhari's *Ṣaḥīḥ* a chapter is entitled: 'Women pray the eclipse prayer with men' followed by a hadith narrated by Asmā' bint Abu Bakr describing her joining that prayer.

Imam Ibn Ḥajar said: 'The way al-Bukhari phrased this heading of the chapter means a rejection of the view of those who disallow this. Al-Bukhari's heading is further confirmed by a different version of the hadith related by Muslim. This version is narrated by Jābir ibn 'Abdullāh and it says: 'He then moved backward and the rows behind him moved backward to the end.' Abu Bakr, Muslim's teacher, said: 'until he reached the women's rows.'

In jihad

Al-Rubayyi' bint Mu'awwidh narrated: 'We used to go with the Prophet on his military expeditions to provide [the fighters] with drinking water and serve them. We also returned the killed ones and the wounded to Madinah.' (Related by al-Bukhari)

In the pursuit of knowledge

Abu Sa'īd al-Khudrī narrated: 'A woman came to the Prophet and said: "Messenger of God, the men have monopolized your teachings. Allocate a day for us when we come and you teach us as God has taught you." He said: "Assemble on such-and-such day at such place." They assembled and he went to them and taught them as God had taught him. He then said: "Any of you, women, who suffers [the death of] three of her children, they will be a shield protecting her from the Fire." One woman said: "How about two, Messenger of God?" She repeated the question twice. He said: "And two. And two. And two."' (Related by al-Bukhari and Muslim)

In enjoining good action

Ibn 'Abbās narrated: 'When the Prophet returned from his pilgrimage, he said to Umm Sinān of the Anṣār: "What stopped you from offering the hajj?" She said: "Abu so-and-so (meaning her husband) had two water carrying camels. He used one to offer the hajj himself and left the other for the irrigation of our farm." The Prophet said: "Performing the 'umrah during Ramadan equals a pilgrimage; or he said: a pilgrimage with me."' (Related by al-Bukhari and Muslim)

In looking after people

Jābir ibn 'Abdullāh narrated: 'The Prophet allowed the Ḥazm family to use the supplication to cure snake bites.' He also said to Asmā' bint 'Umays: 'Why do I see my young nephews so thin? Are they in want?' She said: 'No, but the evil eye affects them.' He said: 'Use supplication [i.e. *ruqyah*] for them.' She said the supplication before him and he said: 'Use this supplication for them.' (Related by Muslim)

In expressing honour and praise

'Ā'ishah narrated that Hind bint 'Utbah said: 'Messenger of God, there was a time when no people on the face of the earth I would have loved to be humbled more than your own family, but today there are no people on the face of the earth I love more to be honoured than your own family.' He said: 'And I, too. By Him who holds my soul in His hand.' (Related by al-Bukhari and Muslim)

In requesting a prayer

Abu Hurayrah narrated: 'A woman came to the Prophet with her baby. She said: "Prophet, pray for this one. (In another version: he is ill and I fear for him.) I have buried three." The Prophet said: "You buried three?" She said: "Yes." He said: "Then you have earned a very strong shield against the Fire."' (Related by Muslim)

In visits

'Ā'ishah narrated: '... When we arrived in Madinah I was ill for a month, and people continued to speak about the false story... As my parents were sitting with me and I was weeping, a woman from the Anṣār sought permission to enter and I admitted her. She sat weeping with me. As we were in this state, God's Messenger came in, said a greeting then sat down...' In another version related by al-Bukhari: 'He praised God and glorified Him, then said: "'Ā'ishah, if you have done something wrong or erred, turn to God in repentance. God accepts the repentance of His servants." She said: A woman from the Anṣār came over and she was by the door. I said: "Are you not ashamed to say this before this woman..."' (Related by al-Bukhari and Muslim)

Kurayb, Ibn 'Abbās's *mawlā* narrated: '... Umm Salamah said: "I heard the Prophet speaking against offering voluntary prayer after the obligatory 'Aṣr Prayer. I later saw him praying them as I had some women from the Ḥarām clan of the Anṣār visiting me. I sent him the maid and said to her: 'Stand by his side and say to him: Umm Salamah says: I had heard you telling people not to pray these two voluntary *rak'ahs* at this time, but I see you offering them now. If he makes a signal with his hand, move away from him. The maid did this and he gave a sign with his hand. She moved away. When he finished, he said: 'You, daughter of Abu Umayyah, have asked about these two *rak'ahs* after 'Aṣr. Some people from the 'Abd al-Qays tribe came to me and I attended to them overlooking the two *rak'ahs* after Ẓuhr Prayer. These are in place of those two."' (Related by al-Bukhari and Muslim)

Umm al-Faḍl narrated: 'A bedouin entered to meet God's Messenger (peace be upon him) as he was in my home. He said: "Messenger of God, I have been married and then married another woman. My first wife claimed that she breastfed my new wife one or two feeds." The Prophet said: "One or two feeds do not block marriage."' (Related by Muslim)

Umm Hāni', the Prophet's cousin, narrated: 'On the day when Makkah was taken over, Fāṭimah sat to the left of God's Messenger and Umm Hāni' to his right. The maid brought a jug of drink and gave it to him. He drank of it then gave it to Umm Hāni' and she drank of it. She said: "Messenger of God, I have broken my fast as I was fasting!" He said to her: "Was it in compensation of a duty fast?" She said: "No". He said: "If it is a voluntary fast, there is no harm."' (Related in *Mishkāt al-Maṣabīḥ*)

Anas narrated that Umm Sulaym used to spread a leather mattress and he would have a nap at her place. When the Prophet was asleep, she would take of his sweat and hair in a bottle and would add it to some perfume.' (Related by al-Bukhari and Muslim)

Imam ibn Ḥajar mentions that Muhammad ibn Sa'd narrated this with a sound chain of transmission, and his version makes clear that this was after the Farewell Pilgrimage.

Qays ibn Abi Ḥāzim reports: 'Abu Bakr was at the place of a woman from the Aḥmus tribe called Zaynab bint al-Muhājir when he noticed that she did not speak. He asked why she did not speak, and he was told that she had pledged to offer the pilgrimage uttering no word throughout her journey. He said to her: "Speak, for such a pledge is unlawful. It is a practice people used to do in the days of ignorance." She started to speak, and she asked him who he was. He said: "I am one of the Muhājirīn." She asked: "Which of them?" He said: "I am from the Quraysh." She again asked: "Which clan of the Quraysh?" He said: "You certainly ask. I am Abu Bakr." She asked: "How long will we maintain this good code which God has granted us after we were in ignorance?" He said: "You will maintain it as long as your leaders maintain the right way." She asked: "What leaders?" He said: "Did your people not have notable figures who would be obeyed when they gave an order?" She said: "Indeed." He said: "These are the ones I mean."' (Related by al-Bukhari)

When making estimates

Abu Ḥumayd al-Sā'idī narrated: 'We went with God's Messenger on the Expedition of Tabuk. When he reached Wādī al-Qurā he saw a woman on a farm. The Prophet told his Companions to estimate the produce of the farm. The Prophet's estimate was ten *wasqs*[12] and he said to her to measure her produce. When we were at Tabuk, the Prophet told us: "There will be a storm tonight. Let no one go anywhere. Whoever has a camel should tie him well. We tied our camels. A storm was blowing. One man rose and the wind threw him at Mount Tayi'. The King of Aylah [a town by the Red Sea] sent the Prophet a gift: a white mule and a cloak. The Prophet wrote to him confirming his status with his people. When he arrived at Wādī al-Qurā [on his way home] he asked the woman: "How much did your farm produce?" She said: "Ten *wasqs*, as God's Messenger had estimated." (Related by al-Bukhari and Muslim)

12. A *wasq* is a measure equal to sixty *ṣā's* and a *ṣā'* is four times the fill of a man's two cupped hands. It is also said that a *wasq* is a camel load.

When visiting ill people

'Ā'ishah said: 'God's Messenger (peace be upon him) visited Ḍubā'ah bint al-Zubayr. He said to her: "Do you want to perform the hajj?" She said: "By God, I am often ill." He said: "Then go for hajj and make a condition. You say: 'My Lord, my place of release [from consecration] is wherever You detain me.'" She was married to al-Miqdād ibn al-Aswad.' (Related by al-Bukhari and Muslim). Ḍubā'ah was the Prophet's cousin as her father was al-Zubayr ibn 'Abd al-Muṭṭalib.

When eating together

Yazīd ibn al-Aṣamm narrated: 'A bridegroom invited us in Madinah. He served us 13 lizards. Some of us ate and some did not. The next day I met Ibn 'Abbās and told him. People around him said many things, and some said that the Prophet said: "I do not eat it, but I do not stop anyone eating it and I do not forbid it." Ibn 'Abbās said: "How bad of you to say that. The Prophet was sent to make things lawful or unlawful. God's Messenger was at Maymūnah's [his wife] and there were al-Faḍl ibn al-'Abbās, Khāid ibn al-Walīd and another woman. A tray of food, with meat, was placed before them. When the Prophet was about to eat, Maymūnah said to him that it was lizard's meat. He withheld his hand and said: 'I never ate this type of meat.' He said to them: 'Eat it.' Al-Faḍl, Khālid ibn al-Walīd and the woman ate of it. Maymūnah said: 'I will not eat anything unless it is something God's Messenger eats.'"' (Related by Muslim)

When nursing

Ḥafṣah bint Sīrīn narrated: '... A woman came over... She told us that her sister's husband was with the Prophet on twelve of his military expeditions, and her sister was with him on six of these. She said: "We nursed the ill and treated the wounded."' (Related by al-Bukhari)

Imam Ibn Ḥajar said that this hadith states several points of interest including the permissibility of a woman treating unrelated men, such as bringing them their medicines and other treatment, which is not physical, unless physical treatment is needed and no temptation is feared.

When giving the pledge of allegiance

Ibn ʿAbbās narrated: 'I attended the Eid al-Fiṭr Prayer with God's Messenger (peace be upon him). The Prophet then stepped down. I can almost see him as he motioned the men with his hand to sit down. He then moved through them until he reached the women and Bilāl was with him. He recited the verse that says: "Prophet! When believing women come and pledge to you that they will not associate any partner with God, nor steal, nor commit adultery, nor kill their children, nor lie about who fathered their children, nor disobey you in anything reasonable, then accept their pledge of allegiance and pray to God to forgive them. God is most-forgiving, ever-merciful." (60: 12) When he finished, he asked them: "Are you in agreement?" Only one woman answered him, saying: "Yes, Messenger of God." He said: "Then, give to charity." Bilāl spread his robe and they threw in it their bracelets and rings.' (Related by al-Bukhari and Muslim)

When seeking the ruler's help

Umm Hāni' bint Abu Ṭālib narrated: 'I went to see the Prophet after Makkah had fallen to Islam. I found him taking a bath and Fāṭimah, his daughter, was screening him. I said my greeting to him. He asked: "Who is this?" I said that I was Umm Hāni' bint Abu Ṭālib. He welcomed me. When he finished his ablutions, he stood up and offered a prayer of eight short *rakʿahs* wearing only one garment. I then said to him: "Messenger of God! My brother, ʿAlī, says that he would kill a man to whom I extended protection. The man is Habīrah's son." The Prophet said: "We will honour your pledge of protection."' Umm Hāni' said that this was in the mid-morning. (Related by al-Bukhari and Muslim)

Zayd ibn Aslam narrated from his father: 'I went out to the market place with 'Umar ibn al-Khaṭṭāb, and a young woman caught up with 'Umar. She said to him: "*Amīr al-Mu'minīn*! My husband has died leaving behind young children. By God they do not have the means to feed themselves, and they have neither a land to till nor cattle. I fear that they may starve. I am Khifāf ibn Īmā' al-Ghifārī's daughter. My father was with the Prophet at al-Hudaybiyah." 'Umar stopped with her for a while, then said: "Welcome to one of close relation." He then went home where he had tied a strong camel. He placed on the camel two sacks which he filled with food, and put in between them some money and clothes. He gave the camel's rein to the woman saying: "Lead him away. You will not have used this up before God brings you something good." A man said: "*Amīr al-Mu'minīn*! You have given her plenty." 'Umar said: "How ill you say! I can see this woman's father and brother besieging a fort for some time then storming it. Then we were counting our shares in it."' (Related by al-Bukhari)

When pleading

Al-Aswad narrated that "Ā'ishah wanted to buy a slave woman called Barīrah. Her masters placed a condition that they would retain her allegiance. 'Ā'ishah mentioned this to the Prophet and he said to her: "Buy her, then set her free. Allegiance is owed to the one who sets a slave free"... The Prophet called Barīrah and spoke to her giving her a choice about remaining married to her husband. She said: "If he would give me this and that I would not stay with him. She chose her freedom."' (Related by al-Bukhari)

Ibn 'Abbās narrated: 'Barīrah's husband was a slave called Mughīth. I can almost see him walking behind her weeping, with his tears wetting his beard. The Prophet said to 'Abbās: "Do you not wonder how Mughīth loves Barīrah and how Barīrah hates Mughīth?" The Prophet said to her: "Perhaps you may go back to him." She said:

"Messenger of God, are you giving me an order?" He said: "I am only pleading for him." She said: "I have no need of him."' (Related by al-Bukhari)

In a case of mutual swearing

Sa'īd ibn Jubayr narrated that he was asked about a married couple who undertook mutual swearing, and I did not know how to answer. 'I went to see 'Abdullāh ibn 'Umar and asked him: "Is the marriage of a couple who undertake mutual swearing terminated?" He said: "Limitless is God in His glory. Yes. The first to ask about this was so-and-so. He said: 'Messenger of God, suppose any of us finds his wife committing adultery: what should he do? If he speaks out, it is very serious; and if remains silent, it is similarly serious.' The Prophet remained silent and gave him no answer. Some time later, the man came again and said to the Prophet: 'I am now afflicted by the question I asked you earlier.' God revealed these verses in Surah 24, Light:

> As for those who accuse their own wives [of adultery], but have no witnesses except themselves, let each of them call God four times to witness that he is indeed telling the truth; and the fifth time, that God's curse be upon him if he is telling a lie. However, punishment is averted from her if she calls God four times to witness that he is indeed telling a lie; and the fifth time, that God's wrath be upon her if he is telling the truth. Were it not for God's favour upon you and His grace, and that God is the One who accepts repentance, the Wise. (24: 6-10)

The Prophet recited these verses before the man, admonished and reminded him that God knows all. He told him that punishment in this present life is much lighter than punishment in the Hereafter. The man said: 'By Him who sent you with the message of the truth I have not told a lie against her.' The Prophet then called in the woman. He admonished and reminded her that God knows all. He told her that punishment in this life is much lighter than punishment in the Hereafter. She said: 'By Him who sent you with the message of the truth he is lying.' The Prophet started with the man and he testified by God four times that he was telling the truth. He coupled his fifth oath with incurring God's curse on himself if he was telling a lie. The Prophet then asked the woman. She testified by God four times that her husband was lying. She coupled her fifth oath by incurring God's wrath on herself if he was telling the truth. The Prophet then ordered the absolute termination of their marriage."' (Related by Muslim)

When enforcing punishment

God says in the Qur'an: 'As for the adulteress and the adulterer, flog each of them with a hundred stripes, and let not compassion for them keep you from [carrying out] this law of God, if you truly believe in God and the Last Day; and let a number of believers witness their punishment.' (24: 2)

ʿAbdullāh ibn Buraydah narrated from his father: 'The Ghāmidī woman came to the Prophet and said: "Messenger of God, I have committed adultery. Purify me." The Prophet told her to go home. The following day, she said to him: "Messenger of God, why do you send me back? Perhaps you are sending me back as you did with Māʿiz! By God, I am pregnant." The Prophet said: "Certainly not now. Go back until you have given birth." When she gave birth, she came back to the Prophet carrying her boy who was wrapped in a piece of cloth. She said: "I have given birth and here he is." The Prophet said: "Go back and breastfeed him, until he is weaned." When she weaned him, she took the boy to the Prophet, with a piece of bread in his hand. She said: "Prophet of God, here he is. I have weaned him and he eats food." The Prophet gave the child to a Muslim man. He then gave instructions and a hole was dug for her up to her chest. He told people to stone her. Khālid ibn al-Walīd hit her head with a stone and some blood sprinkled on his face. He cursed her. The Prophet (peace be upon him) heard him. He said: "Do not curse her, Khālid. By Him who holds my soul in His hand, she has repented in a way which would have ensured the forgiveness of a hardened people's oppressor." He then ordered the funeral prayer for her and she was buried.' (Related by Muslim)[13]

13. The woman was guilty of a crime that carried a mandatory punishment. The rule is that if such a crime – and there are only four such crimes in Islamic law – is confirmed through repeated clear confession or the testimony of the required witnesses, the punishment must be enforced. It cannot be waived.

Scholars' Statements Concerning the Ḥijāb *and its Being Applicable Only to the Prophet's Wives*

- Al-Athram said: 'I said to Abu 'Abdullāh [meaning Imam Aḥmad ibn Ḥanbal]: It appears that Nabhān's hadith quoting the Prophet: "Are you two also blind?" applied to the Prophet's wives in particular, while the hadith concerning Fāṭimah bint Qays, saying: "Stay your waiting period at Ibn Umm Maktūm's home," applies to all people. He said: "Yes."'
- Having related that when Ibn Umm Maktūm entered, the Prophet said to his two wives, Umm Salamah and Maymūnah: 'Go behind the screen,' Abu Dāwūd said: 'This applies to the Prophet's wives in particular. Remember that Fāṭimah bint Qays spent her waiting period at Ibn Umm Maktūm's place. The Prophet said to her: "Stay during your waiting period at Ibn Umm Maktūm. He is a blind man and you can take off your outer garment at his place."'

Commenting on the Qur'anic verse that says: 'Say to the believing men to lower their gaze,' al-Qurṭubī said: 'Assuming that the hadith that says, "Are you two also blind?" is authentic, it only means that it is a strict application to the Prophet's wives in particular because of their status. It is similar to the stricter measure of making the *ḥijāb* applicable to them only, as referred to by Abu Dāwūd and other scholars of eminence.' Al-Qurṭubī is referring here to Abu Dāwūd's statement that it applied to the Prophet's wives in particular.

- Ibn Qutaybah said: 'We say that God, the Mighty and Exalted, commanded the Prophet's wives to stay behind a screen as he ordered us not to speak to them except from behind a screen, as he says: "When you ask the Prophet's wives for something, do so from behind a screen." (33: 53). It is the same if a blind man or a sharp-eyed man enters their place without a screen separating them. All of them would be disobeying God in this case. The Prophet's wives would be in an act of disobedience if they admitted any man, other than those mentioned in Verse 33:55, to enter their place without a screen separating them. This applied to the Prophet's wives only, in the same way that the prohibition of marrying any Muslim applied to them only.
- *Qadi* 'Iyāḍ said: 'The *ḥijāb* obligation applied to the Prophet's wives in particular. It was obligatory to them, without any different view with regard to their faces and hands. They could not uncover these to give evidence or for any other purpose. They were not permitted to appear in person, even if fully covered, except for a necessity, such as going out to relieve themselves. God says: "When you ask the Prophet's wives for something, do so from behind a screen." When they met people, they sat behind a screen. When they went out, they covered themselves totally... When Zaynab passed away, they placed a tent over her bier to cover her.'

> In his commentary on Muslim's *Ṣaḥīḥ*, al-Nawawī quotes *Qadi* 'Iyāḍ's explanation without adding any further comment. Does this mean that al-Nawawī also confirms that the *ḥijāb* applied only to the Prophet's wives? God knows best.
>
> Al-Nawawī also mentions in his commentary: 'Hishām ibn 'Urwah said: "What is meant by 'their need' is that when they needed to relieve themselves, not for general life needs, but God knows best.'

We need to stress that he limits the need to the necessity of answering the call of nature. This limitation applied only to the Mothers of the Believers. No one ever said that women must not go out for their life needs. Otherwise, they would be placed under much hardship.

- Al-Muhallab said: '... The *ḥijāb* applies only to the Prophet's wives in particular.'
- Ibn Baṭṭāl said: '... Muslim women generally are not required to emulate the Prophet's wives with regard to what they were required of staying behind a screen.'

The Applicability of the Ḥijāb *in the Light of the Fundamental Principles of Jurisprudence*

One: The reason for making the *ḥijāb* obligatory on the Prophet's wives

The reason for the *ḥijāb* obligation is stated in the Qur'an as God says: 'When you ask the Prophet's wives for something, do so from behind a screen: this makes for greater purity for your hearts and theirs.' (33: 53) The question here is what sort of purity is meant here? Is it the general purity which is required of all men and women, which includes controlling one's desire? This means facing a small or large measure of temptation and ensuring not to yield to it. This is the purity ensured by the manners Islam requires us to observe when men and women meet. Or is it a special degree of purity that aspires to the same level that exists between a man and his mother? This is a sublime degree of purity that is free from any element of self-control whereby a believer needs to overcome sexual temptation.

We feel that it is this sublime degree that was required in the case of the Prophet's wives. God chose that the Prophet's wives should be Mothers of the Believers, and thus He honoured the Prophet's home ensuring that nothing there would be remotely unbecoming. Thus, the statement in the Qur'anic verse, 'This makes for greater purity for your hearts and theirs,' means that this measure ensures that you do not suffer the temptation that you might normally suffer, and what may come with it, such as looks, thoughts and pleasant conversation. This is not allowed between you and your mothers.

This meaning is further endorsed by what the verse says next: 'Moreover, it does not behove you to give offence to God's Messenger, just as it would not behove you ever to marry his widows after he has passed away. That is certainly an enormity in God's sight.' (33: 53) The fact that it was forbidden for the Prophet's wives to marry anyone else at any time was one reason for their screening. Open meetings may bring about thoughts of marriage to either man or woman. Marriage is a natural relationship which is encouraged by Islam. However, since the Prophet's wives were not allowed to marry anyone other than the Prophet, mixing with them was prohibited and requests put to them had to be made from behind a screen. In other words, the prohibition of marriage necessitated what strengthens disinclination to marry by the Prophet's wives and by Muslim men generally. It also necessitated special measures of protection so that no man saw them and they saw no man, except in very rare circumstances. Thus, they lived the life of hermits. 'Ā'ishah, a Mother of the Believers, was still a young woman when the Prophet passed away, but she remained a widow looking for no new marriage: she died at the age of sixty-six.

Ibn Sa'd writes in *al-Ṭabaqāt al-Kubrā*: 'The Prophet's wives were in mourning for four months and ten days. They would visit each other, but each would be in her own home during the night. They remained unmarried like hermits. Every one of them was heard weeping at least once every two or three days.'

Had the analogy been carried in full, the prohibition of marriage would have entailed the implementation of other rules that apply to those whom one cannot marry, which means the permissibility of revealing charms and adornments, not the obligation of screening. However the analogy was not applied in full. This was due to the fact that the prohibition of marriage in this case was indeed very special. It was based on a purely abstract consideration, which was the special honour given to the Prophet (peace be upon him). Furthermore, it was a prohibition that applied to all male humans of all races and all countries. The prohibition of marrying one's biological or breast-feeding mother is based on material and psychological considerations relating to human nature, and it applies to a small number of people, as it remains within a particular relationship.

To sum up: temptation in this case was possible because the relationship between the Mothers of the Believers and men generally did not include the natural absence of desire that exists between immediate unmarriageable relatives. Therefore, the analogy with normal mothers could not be carried in full. The Prophet's wives were ordered to be totally unobserved, so that men would have a feeling of strong respect and awe when they spoke to them. It also gave the Prophet's wives a motive to elevate themselves above the natural inclination to the other sex. Thus, both sides recognised the status of motherhood which God had assigned to the Prophet's wives as He said: 'The Prophet has more claim on the believers than they have on their own selves; and his wives are their mothers.' (33: 6)

Two: The special status of the *ḥijāb* vis-a-vis other special rules applicable to the Prophet

We can divide rules that applied specifically to the Prophet into two types. The first related to superior actions that enhanced his position with God, such as night worship, fasting continuously for more than one day, abstention from eating from what was given in charity, and refraining from eating bad-smelling food. There may be room for us to follow the Prophet's example in some of these, within the rulings applicable to us in every case.

The other type consisted of relaxing or restricting the legitimate limits applicable to all Muslims. Examples of this relaxation included the permission given to the Prophet to have more than four wives, as God says: 'No blame whatsoever attaches to the Prophet for doing what God has ordained for him.' (33: 38) Another example is that he was given complete freedom as to how he shared his time among his wives. God tells him: 'You may defer any of them you please, and take to yourself any of them you please. No blame will attach to you if you invite one whose turn you have previously set aside.' (33: 51) Examples of restricting legitimate limits included the prohibition of inheritance from the Prophet. None of his children or other members of his family could inherit anything from him. The Prophet said: 'We [prophets] are not inherited. Whatever we leave behind is *ṣadaqah*, i.e. goes to charity.' Another example is that the Prophet was not permitted to replace any of his wives with another woman. God tells him in the Qur'an: 'You [Muhammad] are not permitted to take any further wives, nor to exchange these for other wives, even though you are attracted by their beauty.' (33: 52) Also, his wives had to be behind a screen if someone wanted to ask them something, and they were forbidden to marry anyone after he passed away, as God says: 'When you ask the Prophet's wives for something, do so from behind a screen: this makes for greater purity for your hearts and theirs. Moreover, it does not behove you to give offence to God's Messenger, just as it would not behove you ever to marry his widows after he has passed away.' (33: 53)

In this second type we are not allowed to follow the Prophet's example, because this would mean violating the limits of what God has legislated for the Muslim community, either by expanding the permitted limits or by restricting what He made permissible. We may reflect on how Islamic law imposed a restriction on the Prophet's offspring, denying them the right to inherit from him while no such restriction applies to Muslims generally. On the contrary, it urges Muslims to give in plenty. Sa'd ibn Abi Waqqāṣ narrated: 'The Prophet visited me when I was ill in Makkah... I asked him: "Messenger of God, may I leave all my wealth to charity?" In another version, he gives his reason: "I have only one daughter." He said: "No." I said: "Then one half?" He said: "No." I said: "How about one-third?" He said: "You may, but one-third is plenty. It is better that you leave your heirs rich than leaving them dependants, asking people for charity."' (Related by al-Bukhari and Muslim)

We may also consider how Islamic law imposed special restrictions on the Prophet's wives, requiring them to be always screened and disallowing their marriage after the Prophet died. On this point, we may re-quote Ibn Qutaybah: 'We say that God, the Mighty and Exalted, commanded the Prophet's wives to stay behind a screen as he ordered us not to speak to them except from behind a screen, as he says: "When you ask the Prophet's wives for something, do so from behind a screen." (33: 53)... This applied to the Prophet's wives only, in the same way that the prohibition of marrying any Muslim applied to them only.' By contrast, there is plenty of room for Muslim women generally with regard to undertaking activities, being involved in life affairs and mixing with other people, marrying again after being divorced or widowed, etc. Indeed, Islam facilitates such marriage by shortening the waiting period in some cases, as God says: 'As for those who are with child, their waiting term shall end when they deliver their burden.' (65: 4) 'When they have reached the end of their waiting-term, you shall incur no sin in whatever they may do with themselves in a lawful manner.' (2: 234) In *al-Jalālayn* commentary on the Qur'an, this refers to wearing adornments and encouraging a marriage proposal. Further, God says: 'You will incur no sin if you give a hint of a marriage offer to [widowed] women or keep such an intention to yourselves.' (2: 235) This refers to a hint of an impending proposal given to a widow when she is still observing her waiting period.

It is clear, then, that to restrict what God has made open to His servants, making it unlawful or reprehensible, is not allowed in Islam. God certainly imposed certain restrictions on the Prophet's wives, in a gesture of honouring him. This was a test set by God which those pure and virtuous ladies patiently accepted but other Muslim women would not wish to have. Yet God compensated the Prophet's wives amply for that restriction. In this life, it was sufficient that they were in the Prophet's company and home as his wives, and they were honoured by being associated with him after he passed away. They further earned the noble status of 'Mothers of the Believers'. In the life to come, they will have double reward in addition to being with the Prophet in Paradise. As God willed this type of ruling to distinguish the Prophet and his household from all other people, so as to honour him and enhance his status, emulating him and following his example in such matters is considered a prohibited aspiration akin to the status of prophethood in one of its special characteristics.

Having drawn this division of the special rules applicable to the Prophet and his household we may ask: Does the rule of the *ḥijab* belong to the first or the second type? Undoubtedly it is of the second type because it restricted something that is permissible to all Muslim women and was practised throughout the Prophet's time, namely meeting and speaking to men with no screen separating them. Moreover, it is not an action that is done to draw closer to God. Had screening been a special virtue through which women draw closer to God, the Prophet's Companions would not have thought it too much for the Prophet's slave who was the mother of his child. Nor would they have said when he married Ṣafiyyah bint Ḥuyay: 'If he screens her, she is his wife, but if he does not, she is his slave woman.' In a different version related by Muslim, 'if he does not screen her, she is mother-of-child.' Had the *ḥijāb* been an honourable quality which becomes every woman, the Prophet would have applied it to his slave woman with whom he consorted. Had permanent staying behind a screen been a virtue which women were encouraged to practise, the Prophet would have made sure that he met women, in his own home or in his Companions' homes, from behind a screen. His Companions, men and women, would have been keen to follow his lead. We have already mentioned the evidence confirming the opposite in all this.

We may add that had permanent screening been a virtue to distinguish Muslim society, the Prophet would have taken some measures to ensure its fulfilment, such as:

- Placing a screen between the rows of men and the rows of women in the mosque;
- Assigning a place for women to put their questions and explain their cases to him, which would be away from where men sat;
- Allocating different periods for men and women to perform their *ṭawāf*, and
- The Prophet would not have agreed to pray that Umm Ḥarām joined the naval expedition when she became a martyr for God's cause.

To sum up: if a Muslim woman screens herself permanently, her action will be seen as an attempt to share a distinctive quality of the Prophet's wives, and an aspiration to be on the same level as the Mothers of the Believers. Yet God says of them: 'Wives of the Prophet! You are unlike any other women.' (33: 32). We must distinguish between a woman who screens herself and refrains from marrying again after the death of her husband, permanently, to follow the Prophet's wives' example, and one who does so at a particular time for particular reasons (such as looking after her young children).

The first case represents an aggression against God's law manifested in imposing what He has not imposed and forbidding what He has not forbidden, or at least volunteering what He does not wish us to volunteer for and dislikes what He does not dislike for us. The second case is one of abiding by God's law as it is within the limits of what is permissible which we can take or leave as suits us and as serves our interests in any particular circumstances.

Three: Do the special rules applicable to the Prophet represent an evidence for Muslims generally?

Scholars of legal theory, i.e. *Uṣūl al-Fiqh*, hold different views on this point. One group consider that such special rules do not represent any evidence for Muslims generally. Al-Ghazālī says: 'What is known to be particularly applicable to the Prophet is not evidence in respect of anyone else.' He then adds: 'They say: his action must be described as right, correct and of benefit; otherwise he would not have done it as an act of worship. In response we say that this is generally correct, so that it cannot be described as prohibited. The point here is whether it is applicable to us. What is right, correct and of benefit in the Prophet's case need not necessarily be the same for us. It may be beneficial when it is attached to the quality of prophethood or to some other quality of his. Hence, he differs from us in a number of things that are permissible, duties or forbidden. Indeed, differences in prayer apply to people who are travelling and those in residence, or to a woman during her menstrual period and one who is not. Hence, difference between the Prophet and the rest of the Muslim community is not precluded.'

Al-Shawkānī said: 'The truth is that when the Prophet tells us clearly that something is special to him, whatever it may be, we may not follow his example in that matter except through legislation applicable to us. For example, if he says this thing is a duty for me, recommended for you, we do it because he told us that it is recommended for us, not because it is a duty for him.' Al-Shawkānī also said: 'If he says that something is forbidden for him only, without telling us that it is permissible for us, it is appropriate to refrain from it. On the other hand, if he says that it is forbidden for him, permissible for us, refraining from it is not appropriate, because abandoning what is permissible is not an act of piety.'

Another group of scholars say that the rules specially applicable to the Prophet provide evidence for the rest of the Muslim community. Shaykh Abu Shāmah al-Maqdisī said: '... It is recommended to follow his example in what is duty for him such as the prayers of mid-morning, i.e. *Ḍuḥā*, and Witr. The same applies to what is forbidden to him, such as eating foods with a bad smell and retaining a wife who dislikes his company.'

Such recommended following of his example means that what is special for the Prophet as a duty is considered recommended for the Muslim community, and what is special as forbidden is discouraged for the Muslim community.

However, a review of the special rules applicable to the Prophet shows that the rule stated by the second group is not consistent. It was a special rule that the Prophet was not allowed to exchange his wives for others. Nor was he allowed to marry a woman who did not migrate with him. No one says that it is reprehensible for a Muslim to replace his wife by another woman or to marry a woman who does not wish to migrate with him. The same applies to the prohibition of inheritance for his wives and offspring and the prohibition of his wives marrying anyone after him. These are special rules applicable only to the Prophet. No one says that it is discouraged for Muslims to inherit their relatives, or that a Muslim woman is discouraged from marrying again after her husband dies. Imam al-Ḥaramayn correctly said: 'Most errors by scholars of schools of fiqh occur when they first state a correct meaning but they do not fully examine it to ascertain whether it applies generally or in particular cases.'

Therefore, we are more inclined to say that the first view is the correct one which means that the rules specifically applicable to the Prophet do not provide evidence that they are applicable to Muslims generally. Muslims need to look for the ruling applicable to them on the basis of other and independent evidence.

Let us look carefully at the rule stated by al-Shawkānī: 'If he says that it is forbidden for me, permissible for you, refraining from it is not appropriate, because abandoning what is permissible is not an act of piety.' This rule applies to the question of *ḥijāb*. It is confirmed that the *ḥijāb* applied to the Prophet's wives only, while it is also confirmed that meeting between men and women generally, without *ḥijāb* or screening, is perfectly permissible. This is confirmed by the Prophet's statement, action and approval, and we have provided ample evidence confirming this. It is as if he said: 'For men to meet my wives without a screen separating them is forbidden, but meeting between men and women generally, without a screen, is permissible. Therefore, it is not permissible for Muslim women to permanently refrain from meeting men without a separating screen, following the example of the Prophet's wives. The Prophet strongly reproached the action of people who refrained from something he allowed. Is it permissible for us to refrain from an act of his guidance? However, this does not negate that it is permissible to use a screen sometimes, as we mentioned earlier.

Finally we would like to draw attention to two important matters

The first is that when it has been confirmed that the *ḥijāb*, i.e. remaining behind a screen when speaking to men, applied only to the Prophet's wives, certain conclusions become very clear. The reader needs to bear these in mind when reading the section on Muslim women's participation in social life and the permissibility of uncovering women's faces. The most important of these conclusions are:

- The verse that requires the *ḥijāb*, stating: 'When you ask the Prophet's wives for something, do so from behind a screen,' does not provide any evidence which suggests that it is obligatory or recommended that conversation between men and women should be conducted with a screen separating them.
- The same verse does not provide any evidence to suggest that it is a duty or preferable that a woman should cover her face when she meets men.
- The argument that texts confirming the permissibility of uncovering women's faces or their meetings with men, with unknown dates of revelation, cannot be discounted or ignored on the basis that they might have preceded the verse requiring the *ḥijāb* obligation.

Secondly, the permissibility of a Muslim woman screening herself and the permissibility of her meeting with men remain at the same level. Such permissibility may have any of the five rulings: obligatory, recommended, permissible, reprehensible and forbidden. For more clarity, we say that the original ruling is that both are permissible, but the other rulings may apply in special cases and special circumstances. The following examples show how each of the other rulings may apply.

1. Meeting between men and women is:
    - Recommended in cases of pursuit of knowledge, or helping soldiers fighting for God's cause;
    - Obligatory when giving a testimony, or earning her living, or rescuing someone in difficulty;
    - Reprehensible in cases when the possibility of tempta-

tion appears strong, or in the absence of some Islamic values, and

- Forbidden in cases when temptation is a certainty or when something forbidden occurs, such as one man and one woman being together in a closed place.

2. Remaining behind a screen is:

   - Recommended when the possibility of temptation appears strong without it;
   - Obligatory when temptation is absolutely certain;
   - Reprehensible when it impedes doing what is right, and
   - Forbidden when it prevents doing what is obligatory.

CHAPTER III

The Debate: Must a Muslim Woman Cover Her Face?

People say that the order given to Muslims, 'do so from behind a screen', implies covering the woman's face. It applies to all Muslim women, not only to the Prophet's wives. Our answer is as follows:

1. The text of the relevant verse addresses the Prophet's wives in particular, not Muslim women generally. This is evidenced by the text itself and the context in which the verse occurs. God says: 'Believers! Do not enter the Prophet's homes, unless you are given leave, for a meal without waiting for its proper time. But when you are invited, enter; and when you have eaten, disperse without lingering for the sake of mere talk. Such behaviour might give offence to the Prophet, and yet he might feel too shy to bid you go. God does not shy of stating what is right. When you ask the Prophet's wives for something, do so from behind a screen: this makes for greater purity for your hearts and theirs. Moreover, it does not behove you to give offence to God's Messenger, just as it

would not behove you ever to marry his widows after he has passed away. That is certainly an enormity in God's sight.' (33: 53)

2. The same may be said about usage of the term *ḥijāb* in many hadith texts: it applies to the Prophet's wives only. Here are a few examples:

   - Anas ibn Mālik narrated: 'God's Messenger married and had his wedding. My mother, Umm Sulaym, made a dish of *ḥays*[14] and served it on a stone plate... After having eaten, some people stayed on, engaged in conversation. The Prophet sat down and his wife was sitting with her face to the wall. The Prophet felt uneasy about the situation, so he went out... They then left. The Prophet came in and entered. I was sitting in the front room. A short while later he came out to me and this verse was revealed. The Prophet went out and recited this verse to the people: 'Believers! Do not enter the Prophet's homes unless...' The Prophet's wives were thus screened.' (Related by Muslim)
   - 'Ā'ishah narrated: 'My uncle came over and sought permission to come in. I refused to let him enter until I had asked God's Messenger (peace be upon him)... This took place after we were commanded to remain behind the *ḥijāb*.' (Related by al-Bukhari)
   - 'Umar ibn al-Khaṭṭāb narrated: 'When the Prophet deserted his wives... and this was before they were ordered to be screened.'[15] (Related by Muslim)

14. *Ḥays* is a dish made of pitted dates, dried milk and ghee.
15. It appears that a mistake has been made by one of the narrators. The correct thing is that it was after the *ḥijāb*.

3. Chapter 2 in this volume is devoted to explaining the meaning of the *ḥijāb* and that it applied only to the Prophet's wives, and not to other Muslim women.

★ ★ ★ ★ ★ ★

People say: God says: 'When you ask them for something, do so from behind a screen: this makes for greater purity for your hearts and theirs.' We may draw an analogy here linking covering the woman's face to the *ḥijāb*. When a woman covers her face, her action helps her to grow further in purity, which is commendable for all men and women in all situations.

We have already discussed this in the previous chapter under the subheading 'The reason for making the *ḥijāb* obligatory to the Prophet's wives'.

People say that verse 33: 59 requires the Prophet's wives, daughters and all Muslim women to draw their outer garments over themselves when they go out. As the Prophet's wives have already been commanded to be screened, this other verse means the outer garment should be brought over the woman's face, so that the screening order to the Prophet's wives is generally implemented.

The answer raises the following two points: The *ḥijāb* verse, 'when you ask them for something, do so from behind a screen', requires the Prophet's wives to be separated from men by a screen within their homes. It also requires the Prophet's wives to cover their faces when they go out. Such was the case before the revelation of this verse requiring them to 'draw their outer garments over themselves'.

This new requirement given in this verse applies to all free women, including the Mothers of the Believers. It means that a woman should draw her outer garment over her blouse and head covering.

The reason is stated in the same verse: 'This will be more conducive to their being recognized and not affronted.' (33: 59) Thus, free women will be clearly recognized and distinguished from slave women. No one will then try to harass them.

★ ★ ★ ★ ★ ★

People say: al-Ṭabarī mentions in his commentary, as do others, a report from Ibn 'Abbās and another from 'Ubaydah al-Salamānī suggesting that the verse mentioning drawing their outer garments over themselves means drawing them over their faces, leaving only one eye visible. They add that a report from Ibn Mas'ūd suggests that the verse that requires women 'not to display their charms except what may ordinarily appear thereof', (24: 31) means that a woman shows nothing other than her clothes. They add that taken together, the two verses provide two pieces of evidence confirming that covering women's faces is a duty. What adds more weight to these reports is that Ibn Kathīr quotes them. He normally chooses the most authentic of al-Ṭabarī's reports. Further, some scrupulous contemporary scholars mention that these reports are authentic.

We have several points to make in response:

1. Al-Ṭabarī and others mention other reports that are at variance with those quoted above. With regard to the verse that requires drawing their cloaks over themselves, some reports suggest that it means 'fixing their outer garments over their foreheads'. Other reports suggest that the verse telling women 'not to display their charms except what may ordinarily appear thereof', means the woman's face and hands.

2. These reports are the statements of noble Companions of the Prophet or scholars from the generation that succeeded them, i.e. the *tābi'īn*. Scholars of legal theory and methodology have much

to say about taking rulings from statements by the Prophet's Companions:

- In his book *Ta'wīl Mukhtalif al-Hadith* Ibn Qutaybah al-Daynūrī says: 'There is nothing wrong if Ibn al-Ḥanafiyyah and Ibn 'Abbās, or 'Alī and 'Umar, or Zayd ibn Thābit and Ibn Mas'ūd differ in their interpretations or the rulings they give. What is unacceptable is that they quote two different reports from the Prophet without explanation. As for their own differences, these occur in numerous cases as some act on what they heard; others apply what they think; while others still exercise their own scholarly reasoning. Therefore, they differ in understanding the Qur'an and in many rulings.
- Ibn Taymiyyah says in *al-Fatāwā*: 'As for statements by the Prophet's Companions: if they are in conflict, reference should be made to God and His Messenger. A statement by any one of them is not a final evidence when others differ with it. All scholars agree on this point.'
- In *al-Mughnī*, Ibn Qudāmah says: '... Imam Ahmad discarded the hadith attributed to the Prophet, saying: "Whoever gives a deceased person his final bath should take a bath himself." He justifies his view saying that the hadith is 'stopped' at Abu Hurayrah [i.e. not authentically reported to be said by the Prophet].
- In *Aḥkām al-Qur'an* Abu Bakr ibn al-'Arabī comments on the view expressed by 'Umar and 'Alī that it is a duty to give a slave who contracted to buy his own freedom a portion of what he has to pay. He says: 'If people ask: what will you do with the view of 'Umar and 'Alī? We say: Glory is to Him who gives the final argument only to the one who received His revelations.'
- Al-Ghazālī says in *al-Mustasfā*: 'Anyone who may err or forget and whom we are not certain to be infallible

cannot be treated as an authority. How can such people's statements be taken as proofs when they are liable to make mistakes? How can they be considered infallible without absolutely proven evidence? How can a group of people be considered infallible when they are liable to differ?... They say that if a Companion of the Prophet says something which is at variance with analogy, it can only be construed as based on him hearing a hadith concerning it. In response we say that by saying so you acknowledge that his statement is not a proof; it is the hadith which is the proof. Yet in this case you rely on a mere assumption of the existence of a hadith. By contrast, our basis is the unanimity of the Prophet's Companions to accept the hadith when reported by one person. They accept such a hadith as it is declared to have been heard and transmitted as said, not an assumed hadith whose wording and occasion are unknown. What a Companion of the Prophet says cannot be construed as a clear statement of having heard the Prophet saying it. He might have relied on weak evidence he might have wrongly imagined to be confirmed. A Companion of the Prophet is liable to make such an error. It may happen that a Companion of the Prophet may hold on to weak evidence or an imagined meaning, while he would certainly have stated his authority if it were a definitive text... To treat a statement by a Companion of the Prophet as evidence in the same way as a hadith by the Prophet is to institute a basis for issuing rulings and judgements. This cannot be done without clear authority.'

3. The statement by 'Ubaydah al-Salamānī that women 'leave one eye uncovered' is contrary to the Prophet's approval of a veil that leaves both eyes uncovered. Can we assume that the text of 'Ubaydah's statement is correct when it requires something different from what the Prophet had approved?

4. The fact that Ibn Kathīr mentions some of these reports does not mean that they are definitely authentic. His effort in choosing the best reports is commendable, but he was not very accurate on certain occasions. Exalted is the One who never errs. To give an example: he states a report attributed to ʿIkrimah and al-Shaʿbī saying that a woman must cover herself in front of her paternal and maternal uncles as she does with strangers. This report is contrary to the clearly expressed and authentic sunnah, as mentioned in the hadith narrated by ʿĀ'ishah: 'My uncle through breastfeeding came over and sought permission to come in. I refused to let him enter until I had asked God's Messenger (peace be upon him). When God's Messenger came in I asked him about this and he said: "He is your uncle; admit him."' (Related by al-Bukhari and Muslim) Moreover, Ibn Kathīr cites another report in explaining the verse requiring women to draw their cloaks over themselves. This report states: ''Ikrimah said: "It means that she covers her neck with her cloak, as she draws it over herself." Ibn Kathīr does not attach extra weight to either report.
5. Some scrupulous scholars of hadith confirm the authenticity of the chain of transmission of the report that says, 'they leave one eye uncovered', up to ʿUbaydah al-Salamānī, but at the same time they say that its chain of transmission up to Ibn ʿAbbās is lacking in authenticity. This means that the authentic version is merely a statement by one of the *tābiʿīn*.
6. Al-Suyūṭī said in *al-Durr al-Manthūr*: 'Ibn Jarīr, Ibn al-Mundhir and Ibn Abi Ḥātim related, as did al-Bayhaqī in his *Sunan*, from Ibn ʿAbbās concerning the meaning of "Tell believing women... not to display their charms except what may ordinarily appear thereof": "The apparent adornment is the woman's face, kohl on her eyes, colouring on her hands and rings. She may leave these uncovered before men who enter her house." He then adds: "not to display their charms to any but their husbands or their fathers..." What she displays before these includes her earrings, necklace, bracelets. As for her anklets and what she wears on her upper arm, neck and on her head may be displayed only before her husband.'

In his book *al-Ḥijāb fi al-Kitāb wal-Sunnah*, Shaykh ʿAbd al-Qādir ibn Ḥabībullāh al-Sindī says:

> I researched the chain of transmission of this report attributed to Ibn ʿAbbās and cited by Ibn Jarīr al-Ṭabarī in his commentary on the Qur'an. I concluded that all its narrators are perfectly reliable, but there is something missing in it, because the narrator ʿAlī ibn Abi Ṭalḥah (died 143 AH, 761 CE) narrates from Ibn ʿAbbās although he never met him. The link between them was Mujāhid ibn Jubayr of Makkah. It is well-known that Mujāhid was an eminent, reliable and accurate scholar. This report by ʿAlī ibn Abi Ṭalḥah from Ibn ʿAbbās was accepted by al-Bukhari who mentions it in several places in his *Ṣaḥīḥ* as an 'attached', or *muʿallaq*, because it does not fulfil his conditions of authenticity. This is stated by Ibn Ḥajar in *al-Tahdhīb*. Imam al-Mazzī refers to this report in his biographical note on ʿAlī ibn Abi Ṭalḥah in *Ṭahdhīb al-Kamāl*, saying: 'Its chain of transmission is incomplete, i.e. *mursal*, and attributed to Ibn ʿAbbās. Mujāhid should have been mentioned in between the two.' This report was upheld by the renowned Syrian scholar, Muhammad Jamāl al-Dīn al-Qāsimī, in his commentary on the Qur'an, as did al-Qurṭubī in his commentary and Imam Ibn Kathīr, mentioning it in several places in his commentary. As such, the report is considered authentic and cited by Qur'anic commentators and other scholars. Indeed, the apparent meaning of texts in the Qur'an and the Sunnah, as well as the views of the Prophet's companions and the *tābiʿīn* confirm it. It should be upheld and taken into account.

It is clear that this report attributed to Ibn ʿAbbās implies the permissibility of a woman leaving her face and hands uncovered in front of her male visitors who are unrelated to her. Shaykh al-Sindī is one of those who say that the report suggesting keeping only one eye uncovered, stated by 'Ubaydah al-Salamānī, is also authentic and consider it obligatory for women to cover their faces. The question is: since he confirms the authenticity of this report, why does he and others uphold 'Ubaydah's report and discard this report attributed to Ibn 'Abbās?

In my view, the better way is to reconcile the two reports, for, in fact, they are not mutually contradictory. It is permissible for a woman to keep her face and hands uncovered when men visit her in her home, but when she goes out, she should be distinguished from slave women by drawing her cloak over herself. One way in which this is done is to draw her cloak over her face keeping one eye uncovered. 'Ubaydah al-Salamānī favoured this way, but other scholars, such as Qatādah, Mujāhid and Abu Ṣāliḥ preferred other ways. Qatādah said: 'She ties her cloak over her forehead,' but Mujāhid said: 'They wear a cloak,' and Abu Ṣāliḥ said: 'They use the cloak as a mask.'

★ ★ ★ ★ ★ ★

People say: The Prophet said: 'A woman in consecration must not wear a veil.' The fact that it is not allowed to wear a veil during consecration means that it is the normal practice at other times, which shows that it is obligatory.

Our answer highlights the following points:

- This argument makes an arbitrary conclusion which is contrary to the rules of deduction. The right thing is that the prohibition of something during *iḥrām*, or consecration implies two things: the first is that it was known and used by some women, and the other is that it is permissible at other times, like all other *iḥrām* restrictions such as wearing a turban, cloak, trousers, shirts and shoes.

- To prohibit a type of clothing during *iḥrām* does not necessarily mean that it is normally worn by all people at other times. Shirts and cloaks, for example, were worn by some men, but not all of them. We do not deny that wearing a veil, i.e. *niqab*, was practised by some Muslim women. They were used to it before Islam and continued to wear it after embracing the faith.
- 'Ā'ishah said: 'A woman must not wear a mask during consecration.' This is similar in construction to the hadith that says: 'A woman must not wear a veil during consecration.' Does 'Ā'ishah's statement imply that wearing a mask was the normal practice at other times and, as such, it is obligatory? If so, a mask merely covers the mouth and chin, leaving most of the face uncovered. Do these people approve of this?

★ ★ ★ ★ ★ ★

People say that Asmā' bint Abu Bakr said: 'We used to cover our faces from men and we used to comb our hair before that during consecration.' They state their argument saying that if the noble female Companions of the Prophet used to cover their faces during consecration, i.e. *iḥram*, when they were supposed to uncover their faces, then covering the woman's face at other times is more likely. They add – on the basis of this hadith narrated by Asmā' and similar ones – that since uncovering the woman's face during consecration is a duty as most scholars agree, and since a duty is not abandoned except for something which is more obligatory, then covering women's faces is obligatory. It is for this obligation that the duty of uncovering their faces during consecration is abandoned.

Our answer makes the following points:

- 'We used to cover our faces' should be understood to mean here 'dropping the end of one's robe over one's face.' Unless we take it in this sense, we will have a problem of having mutually contradictory texts which cannot be reconciled. The Prophet (peace be upon him) prohibited wearing a veil during consecration. His noble female Companions would never disobey him and do what he prohibited. Dropping the end of one's robe over one's face is permissible, according to 'Ā'ishah's hadith speaking of what is permissible during *iḥrām*, or consecration: 'A woman may drop her robe over her face if she wants.' She also said: 'Riders might pass by us as we were with God's Messenger in consecration. When they were parallel with us, any one of us may drop her outer garment, from the top of her head over her face. When they were ahead of us, we uncovered.' Also, Ibn al-Mundhir said: 'Scholars are unanimous that a woman may wear all types of tailored garments and shoes, and that she covers her head and hair, except her face. She drops her robe slightly over her face to avert men's looks, but she does not cover her face fully.'

- Asmā''s statement, 'We used to cover our faces,' may be understood to mean that this was only when a group of men overtook them, and there were all sorts of people among them. Some might have stared intently at women causing them some embarrassment, particularly in the crowded time of the hajj, even though they did not cover their faces normally. Indeed, her statement does not definitely mean that she normally used to cover her face when she was not in consecration.
- We need to remember that Asmā' said this to make clear that it is permissible for a woman in consecration to cover her face with the end of her robe. Her statement indicates that such covering might have been occasional or might have been frequent.

If, for argument's sake, we suppose that Asmā' bint Abu Bakr habitually covered her face when she was not in consecration, does this mean that covering their faces is a duty for all women? According to scholars of methodology, the mere action does not indicate a duty; it merely indicates permissibility. We made this clear when we talked about the hadith that says: 'A woman in consecration may not wear a veil.' If some women used to wear a veil during the Prophet's lifetime, others did not and they were in the majority, as we explained in Chapter 3 of Volume 4 of this abridged version.

☙ There may be some hadiths that are similar to Asmā''s hadith implying that some women dropped the end of their garments over their faces, but these hadiths do not mean that those ladies did not discard one duty in order to do what is more obligatory. Their duty was not to cover their faces with a veil or a similar cover. They observe this duty when they drop the end of their garments over their faces, because such an action does not mean covering their faces. It is merely placing a sort of a screen between men's eyes and their faces.

☙ In his book *al-Ḥijāb*, Abu al-Aʿlā Mawdūdī mentions another text that refers to the action of some women in consecration. It adds a piece of information that deserves consideration. Fāṭimah bint al-Mundhir said: 'We used to cover our faces from men when we were in consecration accompanying Asmā' bint Abu Bakr al-Ṣiddīq and she did not object to our action.' If accurately reported, the last part, 'she did not object,' implies that Asmā' herself did not cover her face during consecration. Had she had a cover, her non-objection would not have merited mention. It may be suggested that at the time when these ladies were in company, Asmā' might have been an elderly woman who was allowed to uncover her face, as she herself said: 'We used to cover our faces from men during consecration.' We say that this is possible, and it is also possible that she might have covered her face at times and did not do so at other times. At any rate, the fact that Asmā' did not object to the action of other women clearly indicates that covering women's faces during consecration is only permissible. It cannot be carried further so as to make it a duty. Had it been a duty, the very thought of someone raising an objection would not have occurred. Moreover, had Asmā' felt that covering their faces was recommended for young women, but not elderly ones, she would have commended their action, rather than refrained from expressing an objection.

★ ★ ★ ★ ★ ★

People say that the Prophet said: 'A woman is a covered *'awrah*.' Since she is *'awrah*, she must be covered in full, without excepting her face.

Our answer is as follows:

- The Prophet's hadith, 'a woman is a covered *'awrah*,' refers to the fact that most of her body must be covered, because all her body is *'awrah* except her face and hands. It is not obligatory to cover most of a man's body, because his *'awrah* is the area between the waist line and the knees, or his genitals only. To refer to the larger part of something by using a term meaning the whole of that thing is a well-known way of expression. That this hadith means the majority of the woman's body, not the whole, is confirmed by the numerous texts showing that Muslim women did not cover their faces during the Prophet's lifetime. We have cited many such texts in Chapter 3 of Volume 4.
- In *al-Mughnī*, Ibn Qudāmah says: 'Some of our Ḥanbalī scholars say that all the woman's body is *'awrah*, as the Prophet's hadith says: "A woman is *'awrah*," but she is given a concession to uncover her face and hands because covering them causes hardship.'
- In *al-Sharḥ al-Kabīr*, another scholar called Ibn Qudāmah writes: 'It has been mentioned that the Prophet said: "A woman is *'awrah*"... This applies to all her body, but it is abandoned in respect of her face because of the need to uncover it. It remains in respect of the rest of her body.'
- In *al-Hidāyah* by al-Marghīnānī we read: 'The body of a free woman is totally *'awrah*, except her face and hands, because

the Prophet says: "A woman is a covered '*awrah*." The two excepted parts set a test through uncovering them.' In the annotations to this reference book, it is said: 'The test is that a woman feels the need to uncover these because she must handle things and must uncover her face when giving testimony or being a party in a legal case.'

☙ In al-Bābartī's explanation of *al-Hidāyah* we read: 'It may be said that the Prophet's hadith, "A woman is a covered '*awrah*," applies to all her body and does not make any exception, while excepting the two or three parts on the grounds of a test, is making specification without an express prior indication, and this is not permissible according to our rules. In answer we cite that the Qur'anic verse says: 'tell believing women... not to display their charms except what may ordinarily appear thereof.' (24: 31) This verse was revealed either before or after the hadith. If it was revealed after the hadith, it abrogates its general meaning. If it preceded the hadith, the hadith cannot abrogate any aspect of what God says, because it is singly-reported.'

We have a word to say to those who are of the opinion that a singly-reported hadith which is proven as authentic may abrogate what is *mutawātir*: we need not speak here about any abrogation or discuss whether the Qur'anic verse abrogated the hadith or the hadith abrogated the verse. We say that the application of the hadith is narrowed down on the basis of the rule of methodology concerned with 'general necessity'. On the other hand, and as we mentioned earlier, making a general statement while intending its meaning to apply to the majority, rather than all, of cases is a normal way of expression.

★ ★ ★ ★ ★ ★

People say: Several texts mention that the Prophet's wives and some of the female Companions of the Prophet and the *tābi'īn* women covered their faces. This means that covering a woman's face is either a duty or recommended practice.

Our answer makes the following points:

- That the Prophet's wives covered their faces was due to the fact that it was especially obligatory on them, as God says in reference to them: 'Ask them from behind a screen.' Chapter 2 of this volume is devoted to the *ḥijāb* being obligatory for them only.
- We do not deny that some women covered their faces with a veil during the Prophet's lifetime. Yet their action does not prove that it was a duty or recommended practice. It only indicates that it was permissible.
- If there are a number of texts implying covering women's faces, we have cited texts that are greater in number and enjoy a better degree of authenticity implying not only leaving the woman's face uncovered but also that this was the more common practice in the Muslim society during the Prophet's lifetime. This means that both practices are permissible and that there is no harm if people choose what they believe to serve their interests better. This is something that differs at different times and places.
- Most texts indicating that some female Companions of the Prophet and *tābi'īn* covered their faces appear to refer to events that took place later than the Prophet's lifetime. This indicates that some Muslim women resorted to covering their faces at a later date. This might have been due to certain factors such as:

    i. Certain aspects of weakness of morality started to appear after the Prophet. These aspects were taken as a pretext to impose stricter measures on women. Here are some examples:

- 'Abdullāh ibn 'Umar said: 'I heard God's Messenger say: "Do not stop your women from attending mosques when they ask permission to go there." Bilāl ibn 'Abdullāh said: "By God, we will stop them, so that they would not use that as a pretext to something untoward." His father went up to him, hurling on him such strong verbal abuse as I never heard him use before.' (Related by Muslim) Imam Ibn Ḥajar said: 'Apparently Bilāl said this as he saw the loose practices of some women and was motivated by his sense of honour.'
- Ibn Jurayj narrated: "'Aṭā' said to us when Ibn Hishām ordered that women must not perform the *ṭawāf* alongside men: "How can he stop them when the Prophet's wives performed the *ṭawāf* alongside men?"' (Related by al-Bukhari)
- Ayyūb narrated from Ḥafṣah; she said: 'We used to prevent our virgin women from attending the Eid Prayers... When Umm 'Aṭiyyah came I asked her: "Did you hear the Prophet [say that]?" She said: "Yes, indeed... I heard him say: 'Let virgin women and those who stay behind a screen come out.'"' (Related by al-Bukhari) Imam Ibn Ḥajar said: '... It appears that they stopped young women from going out because of the deterioration of morality after the early period. The Prophet's companions did not take that into consideration, but thought that the ruling continued as it was during the Prophet's lifetime.'

ii. The great expansion of the Muslim state provided an affluent standard of living which made women more stationary at home, going out only occasionally. They no longer needed to attend to their own needs, as they had maids and servants. Perhaps the infrequent need to go out increased the practice of covering women's faces, without difficulty, because it was only done when going from one home to another, which took place at intervals.
iii. The expansion of the Muslim state also led to the emergence of a rich class in the cities. It might have been that subconsciously, this class tried to distinguish itself by its appearance. Thus, they used the veil for distinction while previously most women using the veil were Bedouin women.

★ ★ ★ ★ ★ ★

People say that when the Prophet married Ṣafiyyah, his Companions said: 'If he screens her, she is his wife but if he does not, she is his slave.' This means that a free woman wears the *ḥijāb* so that no one can see her, while a slave does not wear the *ḥijāb*.

We have the following two points in answer:

- The *ḥijāb* in this context means what was applicable to the Mothers of the Believers and it means screening their persons from men. Chapter 2 in this volume is devoted to proving that this was applicable only to the Prophet's wives. Since the Prophet's Companions were fully aware of this fact, they said what they did.
- If, for argument's sake, we say that the *ḥijāb* mentioned in the Qur'anic verse applied to all free women, but not to slaves, Ṣafiyyah, had she been a slave, would have been excepted for

two reasons. The first is that she was pretty, which would have required that she should cover all her body like a free woman. Ibn Taymiyyah said: 'That some women, particularly those who would stir temptation by showing her charms and adornments, should be excepted is certainly more valid.' The other reason is that when a slave woman is chosen to be consorted with sexually, many of the rules applicable to free women become applicable to her. On this point, Ibn al-Qayyim said: '... This applies to slave women who are consorted with. It is the usual practice that they should be protected and should stay indoors. Where do we find an indication that God and His Messenger permitted them to uncover their faces in markets, streets and where people meet?... This is greatly mistaken.'

★ ★ ★ ★ ★ ★

People say: There are many texts indicating the requirement that Muslim women should not be seen by men. One of these is a hadith narrated by Umm Salamah: 'If any woman of you has a slave who has contracted to buy his own freedom and he has enough to settle [what he owes], she should be screened from him.' (Related by Abu Dāwūd)

We have the following point to make in answer:

- In this hadith, the Prophet is addressing his wives, the Mothers of the Believers, and the *ḥijāb* meant here is to have a curtain or screen separating them from men, not the mere covering of their faces. This form of *ḥijāb*, and the very word *ḥijāb*, applied to the Prophet's wives only, not to Muslim women generally, as we explained in Chapter 2.
- That the Prophet's address in this hadith was to his wives in particular is confirmed by several reports which refer to

them in particular. Some of these reports are authentic and contradict the hadith related by Abu Dāwūd, which lacks authenticity. The reports make clear that a slave who has contracted to buy his own freedom continues to have the same rulings as slaves until he has paid his dues in full. Our point here is that all these reports confirm that only the Mothers of the Believers needed to be screened from men.

- Al-Bayhaqī narrated that al-Qāsim ibn Muhammad said: 'Some Mothers of the Believers had a slave who had agreed to buy his own freedom. She would not screen herself from him if he still owed a single dirham. Once he had paid the agreed amount in full, she would put up the screen from him.'
- Ibn Abi Shaybah narrated on the authority of 'Amr ibn Yasār: 'I sought permission of entry at 'Ā'ishah's home, and I raised my voice. She said: "Is that Sulaymān?" I said: "Sulaymān." She asked: "Have you paid off what you owe of your agreed price?" I said: "Yes, except for a small amount." She said: "Come in. You remain a slave as long as you owe something."'
- Al-Ṭaḥāwī narrated on the authority of Sālim, the Naḍarīs *mawlā*, that he said to 'Ā'ishah: 'I think you shall screen yourself from me.' She said: 'What is the matter with you?' He said: 'I have agreed to buy myself.' She said: 'You remain a slave as long as you owe something.'
- Sa'īd narrated in his *Sunan* from Abu Qilābah: 'The Prophet's wives did not screen themselves from a slave who had agreed to buy himself as long as he still owed a single dīnār.'

☙ If, for argument's sake, we take the address to include all Muslim women, then the *ḥijāb* means covering the hidden adornments as stated in the Qur'anic verse: 'Let them... not display their charms to any but their husbands, or their fathers, or their husbands' fathers, or their sons, or their husbands' sons, or their brothers, or their brothers' sons, or their sisters' sons, or their womenfolk, or those whom they rightfully possess.' (24: 31) This verse makes an exception in the case of slaves. If a slave contracts to buy his freedom and actually pays the agreed price, he is no longer a slave. As such, he is removed from the exception and becomes like other men.

★ ★ ★ ★ ★ ★

People say that a hadith mentions that 'A pretty woman from Khath'am came to the Prophet to ask him for a ruling. Al-Faḍl kept looking at her and she looked at him. The Prophet repeatedly turned al-Faḍl's face the other side...' The Prophet's action indicates that it is forbidden to look at women's face. Since such looking is forbidden, women must cover their faces.

In answer we say that this conclusion is arbitrarily made in contradiction of rules of methodology. Casting a hard look and looking fixedly and repeatedly at a woman is agreed as forbidden. The evidence is the Qur'anic verse that says: 'Tell the believers to lower their gaze.' The Prophet says: 'Give the road its right.' They asked: 'What is the right of the road?' He said: '... and lowering one's gaze.' However, there is no direct link between the prohibition of looking and a requirement to cover women's faces. Had covering the woman's face been based on the prohibition of fixed looking, the Prophet would have ordered the woman from Khath'am to cover her face if she was not in *iḥrām*, or to drop the end of her robe over her face if she was in *iḥrām*. However, the Prophet issued neither order to her. Hence, her keeping her face uncovered is not prohibited and its covering is not obligatory.

★ ★ ★ ★ ★ ★

People say that Ibn Taymiyyah said: 'God refers to two types of adornments: one apparent and another which is not apparent. He made it permissible for a woman to leave her apparent adornment uncovered before men other than her husband and immediate relatives who are *maḥram*. Then God revealed the verse that requires the *ḥijāb*, saying: "Prophet! Say to your wives, daughters and all believing women that they should draw over themselves some of their outer garments." (33: 59) He thus placed a separation between men and women... Nothing of women is now permissible for men to see other than their outer garments. Ibn Mas'ūd who says that the apparent adornments mean the outer garments mentions the final case, while Ibn 'Abbās's statement refers to the initial case as he says that the apparent adornments refer to what is on the woman's face and hands, such as kohl and rings.' Ibn Taymiyyah also says: 'According to the more correct of the two views, a woman may not uncover her face, hands and feet before men who are strangers. This is the opposite of what was the case before it was abrogated.'

We will give two points in answer. The first is that we ask: what evidence is there to confirm that abrogation has taken place? Ibn Mas'ūd states: 'The apparent adornments are the outer garments,' while Ibn 'Abbās says: 'It is what appears on a woman's face and hands such as kohl and rings.' These are simply two views of understanding one verse of the Qur'an, which says: 'Let them... not display their charms except what may ordinarily appear thereof.' (24: 31). An explanation of a verse is to mention its meaning after it is revealed, not after the revelation of a different verse that may abrogate it. In other words, it cannot be claimed that Ibn Mas'ūd said the final case and Ibn 'Abbās the former case. Let us remember that if there are two views concerning the meaning of this verse, there are also two views about the meaning of the verse that orders women to 'draw over themselves some of their outer garments.' (33: 59). One says that it means drawing it over the woman's face and the other over her forehead.

Our other point is that Ibn Taymiyyah mentions elsewhere that the verse requiring women to 'draw over themselves some of their outer garments' (33: 59) occurs after the one telling them 'not to display their charms except what ordinarily appears thereof'. (24: 31) This suggests that the first verse abrogated the second. Does the chronological order of the revelation of these verses suggest that verse 33: 59 was revealed after verse 24: 31? The verse that required the Prophet's wives to be screened is verse 33: 53. This verse was certainly before the Falsehood Story. In her narrative of this story, 'Ā'ishah says: 'I travelled with God's Messenger (peace be upon him) after the *ḥijāb* was ordained...' (Related by al-Bukhari and Muslim) The Qur'anic refutation of the Falsehood Story is stated in verses 11-20 of Surah 24. This shows that the verse stating the order 'Tell believing women... not to display their charms except what ordinarily appears thereof' (24: 31) was revealed after the verse requiring them to 'draw over themselves some of their outer garments' (33: 59). In other words, the claim of abrogation is suggesting that the former verse abrogates the later one. Can it be right?

★ ★ ★ ★ ★ ★

People say that Ibn Taymiyyah said: 'Scholars have disputed the question of looking at a woman who is not a *maḥram*... It is said that it is not permissible. This is the apparent view of the Ḥanbalī School which considers that every part of a woman's body, even her nails, is *'awrah*. This is also Mālik's view.' This statement by Ibn Taymiyyah, a highly respected imam, tends to confirm that covering the woman's face is a duty according to the apparent view of Ahmad's School, as also Mālik's School.

Ibn Taymiyyah was undoubtedly a great scholar and an imam in his own right, but everyone makes mistakes. All praise be to God who never errs. We refer the reader to Chapter 5 of Volume 4, as this fully explains the views of the Ḥanbalī and Mālikī Schools regarding the woman's *'awrah*. It also includes a discussion of Ibn

Taymiyyah's statement that 'every part of a woman's body, even her nails, is '*awrah*.'

★ ★ ★ ★ ★ ★

People say that God says: 'Let them not swing their legs in walking so as to draw attention to their hidden charms.' (24: 31) Which is stronger in temptation: swinging a woman's leg and the sound of an anklet or her face?

We give the following two points in answer:

- There is no doubt that there is temptation in a woman's face. However, in His infinite wisdom, God has bypassed this and did not forbid uncovering her face because keeping it uncovered serves various interests, as we have explained in Chapter 4 of Volume 4. Islam forbids the additional elements that stir temptation, such as sharply-delineated makeup and strong perfumes.
- Swinging women's legs is forbidden because, as Abu al-Su'ūd says in his commentary on the Qur'an: 'It stirs men's feelings towards them and suggests that the women doing so are inclined towards men.' Al-Qurṭubī says in his commentary: 'Hearing this type of adornment stirs stronger temptation than seeing it.'

★ ★ ★ ★ ★ ★

People say: The prettiest part of a woman's body is her face. Can it be excluded from the '*awrah* while the '*awrah* includes the bottom aspect of a woman's shins?

We have several points to make in answer:

- Is the '*awrah*, of man or woman, the prettiest part of their bodies? There is something peculiar that makes a certain part of the human body *'awrah*. The *'awrah* starts with the genitals, which are not a pleasant sight to look at. The genitals are the only parts that are unanimously agreed upon to be the man's *'awrah*. Next is the surrounding areas: the abdomen and the thighs. That is the whole of a man's *'awrah*. The same is the woman's *'awrah* in respect of men who are her *mahrams*, i.e. relatives she cannot marry: her father, brother, uncle, nephew. This is according to some scholars, while others extend her *'awrah* with these relatives a little further.

ꕥ When we look at these limits we realise that the *'awrah* first of all relates to the parts of the body that are involved in sexual intercourse and the parts adjacent to these. When one sees these parts, one is reminded of sexual intercourse and desire is stirred. Secondly, the *'awrah* relates to parts of the body men and women do not need to uncover in normal situations, whether inside or outside the home, and whether during work or rest periods. Here we note the wisdom and compassion of the Legislator, as He did not wish to trouble human beings by requiring them to cover the parts of their bodies they need to uncover for various reasons. We outlined these when we talked about the permissibility of keeping the woman's face uncovered in Chapter 4, Volume 4.

ꕥ The woman's *'awrah* with men who are strangers extends much farther, as it includes all her body except her face, hands and feet. This is due to several considerations: 1) God has given the different parts of the woman's body a special type of beauty that is especially attractive to men; 2) her work is mostly looking after the family home and taking care of her children. Thus she can put on the sort of clothes she likes, without difficulty; and 3) she has only a limited need to meet men who are unrelated to her. If she has such need and if she deals with men, covering herself is not too hard for her.

ꕥ What is more important than all this is to say that Islam always looks at ways to ensure that temptation does not occur, and tries at the same time to remove difficulty and hardship. In the question of uncovering the woman's face, Islam attaches more weight to the rule of removing difficulty and hardship than to preventing temptation. It considers temptation in this case to be limited.

★ ★ ★ ★ ★ ★

People say that many scholars consider it obligatory for women to cover their faces so as to prevent the cause of temptation.

We have several points to make in answer:

1. This is the view of some scholars based on their own scholarly reasoning and aimed to prevent temptation. As such, it is not the basic ruling of the Legislator concerning covering or uncovering the woman's face. God has made it obligatory to cover the *'awrah* only. What is not *'awrah* is not required to be covered in the first place. Yet a scholar may act on the basis of his reasoning and rule that it is recommended or a duty to cover the woman's face, even though it is not part of the *'awrah*, in a particular situation. This ruling may be right or wrong, according to the evidence the scholar uses as a basis for his reasoning. On the other hand, this ruling may be looking at a particular interest relevant to a particular period of time.
2. There are many types of temptation in life, and the most serious of these are those of women, wealth and children. God says in the Qur'an: 'Alluring to man is the enjoyment of worldly desires through women and offspring, heaped-up treasures of gold and silver.' (3: 14) Yet although these three are the most serious temptations, people cannot do without them. Money, for example, is perfectly legitimate to start with, and it is essential for human life. Indeed, life cannot be sustained without it. Therefore, we cannot prohibit this legitimate necessity, stopping

it from fulfilling its role in building life on earth on the basis of preventing the cause of temptation. Yet, we agree that it has strong temptation. Some Sufis did actually forbid themselves dealing with money, abandoning all that relates to this world and preferring to live in their hermitages. This is not permissible in Islam. What we should rather do is prohibit the aspects Islam prohibits concerning money and how it is earned and spent. The same may be said about women: to deal and interact seriously with them in all spheres of life is permissible. Indeed, such serious dealing is one of life's essentials. Without it, life cannot be sustained. However, when a woman covers her face, this is coupled in most, though not all, cases with neglecting social life in order to stay away from men and not to deal with them. Thus, covering the woman's face seems to make a strong plea towards avoiding men and staying away from them, except, perhaps, when face covering leaves an opening for the woman's eyes as some Bedouin women do these days. The veil, or *niqab*, was used prior to Islam and in the early Islamic period by some women, particularly Bedouins. It was considered a type of clothing that shows beauty while providing cover. It does not prevent Bedouin women from dealing with men in normal life matters, in the same way that a full dress and head covering, which Muslim women wear nowadays in some countries, causes no impediment to interaction between them and men.

3. God, the Legislator, warns against the temptation posed by women. This is a warning that requires keeping the natural inclination towards women under control, so that it does not lead to unlawful behaviour starting with a forbidden look, speech or touch, or what is more serious, leading ultimately to fornication and adultery. The Legislator, who knows His creation and their nature, points out in detail what stirs temptation and lays down a set of rules to control them:

   - Fixed looks stir temptation for both men and women. Hence, God gives the same order to both: 'Tell believing men to lower their gaze.' (24: 30) 'Tell believing women to lower their gaze.' (24: 31)

- Revealing inner adornments also stirs temptation, and God commands: 'Tell believing women... not to display their charms except what ordinarily appears thereof.' (24: 31)
- Temptation may be stirred by wanton movement or the sound of anklets. Hence, the command: 'Let them not swing their legs in walking so as to draw attention to their hidden charms.' (24: 31)
- Soft speech may be tempting. Moreover, wanton, unrestrained speech could lead to terrible results. Hence, God says: 'If you truly fear God, do not speak too soft, lest any who is sick at heart should be moved with desire; but speak in an appropriate manner.' (33: 32)
- To put one's hand out to shake hands with women generally may stir desire.[16] Hence, the Prophet says: 'I do not shake hands with women.' Also his guidance is summed up in: 'His hand never touched a woman's hand in accepting their pledges of allegiance.' (Related by al-Bukhari and Muslim)
- Places crowded with men and women may arouse desire. Hence, the Prophet's guidance shows that 'when he finished his prayer, he stayed in place for a short while so that women could leave before they were caught up by men.' (Related by al-Bukhari) He said: 'You may not walk in the middle of the road.'
- Desire is aroused when a man is alone with a woman in a private place. Hence the Prophet orders: 'Let no man be alone with one woman.' (Related by al-Bukhari)
- Strong perfume women wear may also arouse desire. Hence, the Prophet said: 'When any woman of you comes

16. In certain situations and when needed, shaking hands with the other sex has a different ruling. This is discussed in Chapter 2, Volume 2. – Author's note.

to the mosque, she should not wear perfume.' (Related by Muslim)

- To frequent suspicious places may stir temptation. The Prophet says: 'Abandon what raises doubts.' (Related by al-Tirmidhī and al-Nasā'ī)

Thus, Islam tries to contain all temptations from all corners, so that Muslim society remains healthy and on the right course.

We conclude that women's serious participation in all spheres of life, wearing decent clothing and with faces uncovered, is perfectly lawful and good. It is essential for a goodly and serious life. We cannot prohibit what is lawful and prevent it from playing its role in building human life. This means that we may not prohibit the presence of women, with their faces uncovered, under the pretext of preventing the cause of temptation. Although such presence and uncovering of faces gives rise to temptation, God, in His absolute knowledge and infinite wisdom permitted them as an act of His grace which He bestows on His creation in order to remove their difficulty. This is a test to which God subjects human beings, men and women, in the same way as He tests them with wealth and offspring. This test is confirmed by what we see of the temptation in societies where women generally cover their faces. It is not any less than temptation in societies where women do not cover their faces. We are speaking about men's feelings, particularly young men, and their inclination towards women and trying to have some sort of relationship with them. It is always the case that the strong think of a legitimate relationship, while the weak always think of an illegitimate one that tries to violate restrictions.

Such a test involving desire can only be countered by a mixture of resistance and patience. Without these two, man becomes weak and fragile. He would fail even at the first test, whether he is tested with riches, children or women. However, we need to bear in mind the things that may accompany the presence of women but God has prohibited because they arouse desire, but He does not consider the uncovering of the woman's face one of these. Therefore, He permits the uncovering of the woman's face as perfectly natural, in the same way as he permits and considers mixed dealings between men and women. At the same time, God prohibits what may arouse desire when added to the uncovering of the woman's face, such as too much makeup and adornments on faces and clothing, as also wearing strong perfumes. He also prohibits practices that may arouse desire and that accompany mixed dealings, such as soft speaking, leg-swinging, crowding and being alone with one person from the opposite sex.

4. The rule of 'preventing the cause' of evil is correct. It means that a permissible action is ruled unlawful if it will, most probably, lead to an evil result, and if implementing this rule ensures the prevention of evil or trouble. We need to ask, however: Did the temptation of women exist during the Prophet's lifetime? We believe that it did, and the evidence for our belief is the Qur'anic verses: 'Say to believing men to lower their gaze,' (24: 30) and 'God is well aware of the most stealthy glance.' (40: 19) Moreover, many hadiths urge believers to lower their gaze. Other hadiths state that some of the Prophet's Companions yielded to the type of unlawful gaze. One of these hadiths is that which mentions the pretty woman from Khath'am at whom al-Faḍl ibn 'Abbās kept looking at. Another hadith mentions a pretty woman who used to come to the mosque and some men tried to offer their prayer in the back rows so that they could look at her.

Yet despite the presence of temptation, God only ordered believers to lower their gaze, but did not command women to cover their faces. There is no difference between pretty and plain women, because temptation occurs in all situations. Some of the female Companions of the Prophet were pretty and others were plain or not so pretty. Yet, God did not make any distinction in the relevant ruling. He left this temptation without closing the door leading to it, as an act of grace, and to give believers room to interact. Therefore, this needs to remain the same, open without further restriction. This is what behoves us to do if we truly believe in His wisdom and we submit to His law. This being the case, how can we operate the rule of 'preventing the cause' in order to block a temptation that has always been in existence. It was well-known to God and He knows its serious effects but He did not block it. To operate the rule of 'preventing the cause' appears in this case as if it aims to supplement what God, the Legislator, left undone. Far be it from us to entertain any such thought.

5. It is true that the problem of temptation is old and was in existence at the time when Islamic law was being revealed, but what is new is that it has increased manifold. Men have neglected God's instruction to lower their gaze. Now they look hard at women's faces. This stirs men's desire and offends Muslim women. So what is the solution? We look to the Prophet's Sunnah for the answer. When he saw that al-Faḍl kept looking at the pretty woman, the Prophet did no more than turn al-Faḍl's face away from her. The Prophet did not order the woman to draw the end of her cloak over her face if she was in consecration, or to cover her face with a veil if she was not. The Prophet's attitude was significant in several ways:

First, it confirms the permissibility of the woman leaving her face uncovered and that it is men's duty to strive against temptation and to lower their gaze. Such striving, at whatever level, is the positive way of resisting the temptation presented by the uncovering of women's faces. To force women to cover their faces is no more than a useless attempt to run away from the temptation which remains present even if all women were to be totally secluded.

Secondly, the Prophet's attitude shows that Muslim society actually enjoins whatever is right and denounces evil. It cooperates to remove evil, physically if possible, but if it cannot then by speaking out against it. If this is also impossible, then by gestures expressing disapproval, such as a disapprobation look, turning one's face away or an expression of disgust. If none of all this is feasible, then it feels the rejection at heart and moves away from that place if at all possible.

Thirdly, the meaning of the text, as well as Islamic legal rules, indicate that Muslim society should always cooperate to remove what is evil. What cannot be achieved in full is not abandoned in total. This means that when verbal admonition and silent disapproval are not effective in removing evil, and it continues to occur here and there, then some arrangements should be put in place to reduce such incidents. Here are some examples of such arrangements:

- Reducing the possibility of repeated looks as much as possible. This is achieved through reducing the frequency of a woman's going out or reducing the time she remains out. Also, women may select the safer places and go out in the company of their immediate relatives. What is important to realise is that this aim must not be achieved through complete separation between men and women or through forcing women to always keep their faces covered. This is contrary to human nature on the one hand, and it may lead on the other to an increase in what is forbidden as some people may resort to dishonest ways to achieve their purpose.
- Providing, when necessary, a special area for women when they share the same occasion with men. This helps to reduce exchanged glances.

Apart from that, passing looks continue to be cast as men and women walk around. Wrong as these are, there is no way other than to tolerate them with patience. At the same time, we need to continue our efforts to educate people and encourage them to do what is right and to shun and refrain from what is wrong.

Thus we realise that the increased temptation in our present time does not allow us to enforce the rule of 'preventing the cause', because the result of the woman uncovering her face is no more than casting a look or several looks at her. It is not a question of fearsome evil or serious risk, amounting to illegitimate sex or what is close to it. This only occurs in rare cases. The rule of 'preventing the cause' does not lead to prohibiting what is lawful unless the continuity of that lawful thing leads to what is forbidden in the majority of cases.

6. When a Muslim woman is irritated by repeated looks on occasions, and if she thinks that this may lead to some serious consequences, it is always open to her to cover her face by drawing the end of her head cover over it. She, thus, effectively removes harm and prevents what is unlawful. To resort to the extreme of issuing a general ruling ordering all women to cover their faces in order to prevent the cause is something that the rule itself does not approve of.
7. We will devote Volume 6 of this series to the debate about the rule of 'preventing the cause' and its exaggerated application. This volume will, God willing, be useful in clarifying issues related to women's participation in social life and also to the uncovering of women's faces.

★ ★ ★ ★ ★ ★

People say that when men meet women who keep their faces uncovered, men do look at them although they are commanded to refrain from this.

We have the following points to make in answer:

1. The order to lower one's gaze means not to cast fixed looks. It cannot mean total avoidance of looking. There are numerous pieces of evidence confirming this, including the Qur'anic orders:

   - 'Tell believing men to lower their gaze' (24: 30) and 'Tell believing women to lower their gaze.' (24: 31). In his explanation of these verses, al-Ṭabarī said: 'If a person sees what it is unlawful for him to look at, he lowers his gaze so as not to look at it. No one can totally close his eyes. Hence, God tells believers to lower their gaze. This means that when a person sees some *'awrah* or something that is unlawful for him to enjoy, he lowers his gaze. If what is being seen is not *'awrah* and the look is not coupled with desire and enjoyment, then there is no harm.' In his commentary, Abu Ḥayyān said: 'A man looks at the face and hands of a woman. He can hardly ever guard against such looks.' Ibn Daqīq al-'Īd said: 'The order uses the preposition *min*, which means "a portion of". Thus, the verse means lowering one's gaze somewhat. It does not mean closing one's eyes totally.'
   - Ibn 'Abbās said: 'Nothing illustrates minor sin better than what Abu Hurayrah narrates from the Prophet (peace be upon him): 'God has assigned to each human being his share of adultery which he will inevitably have. Adultery by one's eye is its looks; by one's tongue its words; the soul desires and feels the urge; and the genital either confirms or belies all this.' (Related by al-Bukhari and Muslim) This hadith is clear in stating that what is forbidden is a look coupled with desire. This is the meaning conveyed by the Prophet's words: 'the soul desires and feels the urge.' It means that looks without desire do not incur a sin. Ibn Baṭṭāl said: 'The hadith calls looks and words 'adultery'

because they lead to full adultery. Hence, the Prophet concludes by saying, 'the genital either confirms or belies all this.' We consider that what leads to the complete act of adultery is a look coupled with felt desire.

Commenting on the hadith mentioning the Khath'amī woman, Ibn Baṭṭāl said: 'The hadith orders lowering one's gaze so as to guard against temptation. It, thus, implies that where temptation is not feared, it is not prohibited... This is confirmed by the fact that the Prophet did not turn al-Faḍl's face the other way until al-Faḍl had continued to look at her for a long time, because he admired her beauty. The Prophet feared the consequences for him... The hadith further implies that the divine order, "Tell believing men to lower their gaze", states an obligation in as far as the rest of the woman's body is concerned.'

I should add that the hadith also implies that when men look at a woman, she is not under an obligation to cover her face. Had this been obligatory, the Prophet would have ordered the woman to cover her face, using a veil or something similar if she was not in consecration, or drawing the end of her robe over her face if she was.

A man asked Ibn 'Abbās: 'Have you attended the Eid Prayer, whether *Aḍḥā* or *al-Fiṭr*, with God's Messenger?' Ibn 'Abbās said: 'Yes. Had it not been for my relation to him, I could not – he was referring to his being young. God's Messenger came over, led the prayer and then delivered a speech. He did not mention any *adhān* [i.e. the normal public call to prayer] or *iqāmah* [i.e. the announcement of starting the prayer]. He then went to the women, admonishing and reminding them. He ordered them to give *ṣadaqah*, or charity. I saw them reaching to their ears and necks, giving Bilāl. He then went with Bilāl to his home.' (Related by al-Bukhari)

Imam Ibn Ḥajar said: 'The evidence the hadith provides is that Ibn ʿAbbās saw what the women did at the time. He was young and they did not cover themselves from him. As for Bilāl, he was a slave. This explanation is stated by some commentators, but it is questionable because Bilāl was a free man at the time. The answer is that it may be that in this case he did not see them with uncovered faces. Taking the hadith at its face value, some Ẓāhirī scholars said: "It is permissible for an unrelated man to see the face and hands of an unrelated woman. As Jābir related the hadith and Bilāl spread his robe to take their donations, this cannot be done without their faces and hands being seen.'

Ibn Ḥajar's answer that 'it may be that he did not see them with uncovered faces' is countered by what Jābir mentions in his narration: 'A woman with dark-red cheeks stood up in the midst of the women...' This description of the woman makes it absolutely clear that her face was not covered. Moreover, the claims that Ibn ʿAbbās was young and Bilāl was a slave and for these reasons the women did not cover their faces from them are countered by the fact that the hadith was narrated by Abu Saʿīd al-Khudrī, ʿAbdullāh ibn ʿUmar and Abu Hurayrah, in addition to Jābir's narration.

- Fāṭimah bint Qays reports that Abu ʿAmr ibn Ḥafṣ irrevocably divorced her ... She came to the Prophet and told him. He said: 'He does not owe you maintenance.' He told her to stay with Umm Sharīk [during her waiting period]. He then told her: 'Umm Sharīk is frequently visited by my Companions.' In another version, he said: 'Do not do that. Umm Sharīk receives many guests. I dislike that your head cover may drop or your robe may be lifted and expose your legs, which lets people see of you what you dislike to be seen. Observe your waiting period at Ibn Umm Maktūm.

He is a blind man and you can put off some of your garments at his place.' (Related by Muslim)

The hadith shows that the Prophet was not concerned about the many guests seeing the woman, but he was concerned about the hardship suffered by the woman if she had to wear her full dress and head covering throughout the day. She may unintentionally have some parts of her body exposed when she rather needed to remain fully covered and this for a long while. Hence, the Prophet said to her: 'I dislike that your head cover may drop or your robe may be lifted and expose your legs, which lets people see of you what you dislike to be seen.'

As the Prophet advised Fāṭimah to observe her waiting period at Ibn Umm Maktūm's home, he was not concerned about his being unable to see her face as he was blind. He wanted to make it easier for the woman to take off some of her clothes, without a problem. On this point, Ibn Daqīq al-'Īd says: 'It is possible to say that he mentioned the man's blindness because she would be able to take off some of her clothes without him seeing her.'

- Durrah bint Abu Lahab narrated: 'I was at 'Ā'ishah's when the Prophet came in. He said: "Bring me water for *wudu* [i.e. ablution]." Both 'Ā'ishah and I reached for the pitcher and I was ahead of her. I took it and the Prophet performed his ablution. He then lifted his eyes to me and said: "You belong to me and I belong to you."'
- Qays ibn Abi Ḥāzim narrated: 'We visited Abu Bakr when he was ill. There was with him a white woman, with painted hands, and she was keeping the flies away from him. She was Asmā' bint 'Umays.'

These two hadiths imply that it is permissible for men to look at women if their looks are not coupled with desire.

2. We now quote what some eminent scholars have said, stating that looking at a woman without desire is permissible:

Mālikī scholars

In *al-Muwaṭṭa'*: Mālik was asked: 'Can a woman eat with a man who is not her *maḥram* [i.e. a close relative she cannot marry], or with her slave?' Mālik said: 'There is no harm in that... A woman may also eat with her husband and whoever is eating with him.' The author of *al-Muntaqā Sharḥ al-Muwaṭṭa'* said: 'This means that it is permissible for a man to look at a woman's face and hands, because these are apparent when one eats with her.'

In *al-Tāj wal-Iklīl li Mukhtaṣar Khalīl*: 'In *al-Mudawwanah* we read: "If a man divorces his wife a third time and banishes her, she should not let him see her face if she can." This may suggest that an unrelated man may not see a woman's face, but it is not so. The order is that she does not let him see her because his intention is to have the pleasure of gazing at her. It is reprehensible for an unrelated man to look at a woman for pleasure because this involves ill-feelings... A woman's face and hands are not part of the *'awrah*, and they are permissible to be seen by anyone, without ill-intention. To look at a woman with desire is forbidden, even if she is fully dressed. Needless to say, it is more so when looking at her face.'

Ḥanafī scholars

In *al-Mabsūṭ* by al-Sarakhsī, a statement makes clear that it is permissible for an unrelated man to see a woman's face. This comes in the context of how to prepare for burial of a woman who dies when she is attended only by men who are unrelated to her. Normally a deceased person is given a bath before the body is prepared for burial. In this case, the men are not allowed to give her a bath, but one of them may perform her dry ablution, i.e. *tayammum*, which involves wiping her face and arms with one's dusted hands. In this case, al-Sarakhsī says: 'If the man is unrelated to her, he performs the dry ablution, using a piece of cloth with which he wraps his hand [so that he does not touch her body]. He turns his face away from her arms, but not from her face, because during her life, a man may not look at a woman's arms.'

Ḥanbalī scholars

Ibn Qudāmah says in *al-Mughnī*: The *Qadi* said: 'It is forbidden for a man to look at any part of a woman's body other than her face and hands, because it is *'awrah*. It is permissible, but discouraged, for him to look at her if he feels no temptation and he looks without desire. This is the view of the Shāfi'ī scholars, based on God's order 'Let them... not display their charms except what may ordinarily appear thereof.' (24: 31)... Moreover, her face is not part of her *'awrah*. As such, it is not forbidden to look at normally, in the same way as a man's face.'

In Ibn Taymiyyah's *al Fatāwā*: 'Scholars have disputed the question of looking at a woman who is not a *maḥram*. It is said that it is permissible to look without desire at her face and hands. This is the view of Abu Ḥanifah and al-Shafi'i, and one view in Ahmad's School [i.e. the Ḥanbalī School].'

3. Having cited all this evidence, we wish to add that some people are strong while others are weak. A strong man is not swayed by the woman's face being covered or uncovered. He is striving in all situations. When looking at a woman who covers her face, he strives against his evil thoughts, and when he looks at a woman with her face uncovered, he strives to lower his gaze. A weak man yields to his own desire and looks hard at an uncovered face. Likewise, he yields to his desire when a woman's face is covered, allowing his bad thoughts to run their course. He may even resort to tricks and look through holes and windows, seeing more than the woman's face. Indeed, the question goes further than this.

Some women are also strong and some weak. A strong woman may be keen to always cover her face, while a weak woman may yield to her own desire and uncover her face at times in order to attract men's looks. When this happens, a weak man succumbs to the temptation and even a strong man may not be fully safe, due to the element of surprise in such a situation and the strong desire it generates.

4. Finally, we add our voice to Ibn Taymiyyah as he says: 'The forbidden looks are looking at people's *'awrah* and looking with desire, even at what is not *'awrah*.' We also join al-Kamāl ibn al-Hammām of the Ḥanafī School who says: 'Looks are permissible on condition that desire is dormant and what is looked at is not *'awrah*.'

★ ★ ★ ★ ★ ★

People say that covering the woman's face is a most effective way of dealing with the desire to stare at women. God knows that human beings are weak and that they succumb to their desire. Apart from the few who are strong in faith, they will not heed the divine order to lower their gaze.

Our answer makes the following points:

- If the order to lower people's gaze is insufficient to deal with the temptation presented by women, and if covering women's faces is the most effective way, why does God, the Legislator, focus on lowering people's gaze, paying no attention to the more effective solution?
- The fact that Islam orders lowering people's gaze means that it finds the alleged effective solution, which is covering women's faces, to present difficulty and hardship. Therefore, God, in His infinite wisdom, determined to remove the difficulty and not to require Muslim women to undertake the hardship of covering their faces.

- Besides, the claim that covering the woman's face effectively counters the desire to look at women is not really true. It may be effective with devout and strong men, but it stirs the curiosity of the weak. A strong and chaste woman may use it to maintain her status, but a weak woman may trifle with it or partly remove it to tempt men.

★ ★ ★ ★ ★ ★

People say that the hadith narrated by 'Ā'ishah: 'When a woman attains puberty, no part of her should be seen except this, pointing to his face and hands,' is lacking in authenticity. Abu Dāwūd said that it is *mursal*, as the narrator Khālid ibn Durayk was not 'Ā'ishah's contemporary. As such, this hadith may not be cited as evidence supporting the permissibility of leaving the woman's face and hands uncovered.

In answer we say that on its own, the hadith is lacking in authenticity. Yet it is narrated with different chains of transmission which give it further support. This is clarified by Shaykh Nāṣir al-Dīn al-Albānī, an eminent contemporary Hadith scholar, in his book *Ḥijāb al-Mar'ah al-Muslimah*. He includes it in his selection of authentic hadiths related by Abu Dawud in his *Sunan*. Of old, al-Bayhaqi provided further evidence to strengthen this hadith, in a different way.[17]

Moreover, had we relied on this hadith alone in stating the permissibility of uncovering the woman's face and hands, our opponents would be right to object. In fact, we rely on a large number of Qur'anic verses and hadith statements, in addition to a set of further evidences and indications. With all this we point out the agreement of early scholars on this point, as this is clear in their own books, though not

17. This is explained by al-Albānī in *ḥijāb al-Mar'ah al-Muslimah* and he gives further details in later editions of the book which he published under the title *Jilbāb al-Mar'ah al-Muslimah*. – Author's note.

the books of recent scholars. We have cited these in Chapters 2, 3, 4 and 5 of Volume 4 of this series.

★ ★ ★ ★ ★ ★

People say that al-Ṭabarī says in his commentary on the Qur'an: 'God, the Exalted, orders His Prophet to say to his wives, daughters and Muslim women generally that they must not dress like slave women when they go out for their needs uncovering their hair and faces. They must draw their outer garments over themselves so that no wicked person harasses them verbally as he realises that they are free women.'

In answer we say:

- Al-Ṭabarī mentions that slave women used to uncover their hair and faces. This does not mean that free women must cover their faces to distinguish themselves from slave women. They will be distinguished if they cover their hair and a part of their faces, by drawing their outer garments over their heads and foreheads.
- This possibility is strengthened by what al-Ṭabarī says when explaining the verse that says that women 'must not display their charms except what may ordinarily appear thereof' (24: 31). He says that the exception refers to the woman's face and hands. He also states that scholars are unanimous that a woman must keep her face uncovered when she prays. We have already proven that the *'awrah* is the same in prayer and other situations. (For details, reference may be made to Chapter 5, Volume 4.)
- It may be that al-Ṭabarī refers here to the possibility of free women covering their faces according to the report by Ibn 'Abbās and 'Ubaydah saying that 'they covered their faces, leaving only one eye.' Al-Ṭabarī did not give more weight to either report: this one or the report that says that they drew their cloaks over their foreheads.

★ ★ ★ ★ ★ ★

People say that Imam Ibn Ḥajar said in his explanation of the hadith that says: 'May God bestow mercy on the early women migrants. When God revealed: "Let them [i.e. Muslim women] draw their head-covering over their bosoms," (24: 31) they tore up their cloaks and used them as covering: "using them as covering" means that they covered their faces.'

Our answer makes the following points:

- With all due respect to Ibn Ḥajar as a great scholar, his statement is not right. The Arabic word used here 'using as covering' is *ikhtamarn*, which is derived from *khimār*. In all books of reference in the fields of Arabic language, Qur'anic commentary and Fiqh, the *khimār* refers to head covering. Therefore, *ikhtamarn* means they covered their heads, not their faces. Indeed, there is plenty of evidence in hadith texts confirming this meaning. Here are some examples:

  - Bilāl narrated: 'God's Messenger wiped over the *khuffs* and the *khimar*.'
  - Mālik narrated from Nāfiʿ that he saw Ṣafiyyah bint Abi 'Ubaydah, Ibn 'Umar's wife, lifting her *khimar* and wiping her head with water. Nāfiʿ was young at the time.
  - Maymūn ibn Mihrān narrated: 'I visited Umm al-Dardā' and saw her covering her head with a thick *khimār*, drawing it over her eyebrows.'
  - Umm 'Alqamah narrated: 'I saw Ḥafṣah bint 'Abd al-Raḥmān ibn Abu Bakr when she entered 'Ā'ishah's home wearing a thin *khimār* showing her forehead. She tore it and said to her: "Do you not know what God has revealed in Surah 24, Light?" She then called for a *khimār* and gave it to her.'

- In his further comments on the hadith, Ibn Ḥajar mentions what confirms that the *khimār* does not cover the face. He says: 'The way this is done is that the woman puts the *khimār* on her head and draws it from her right side over her left shoulder. This is wearing a head cover. Al-Farrā' said: "In pre-Islamic days, a woman used to drop her *khimār* behind her and leave the front uncovered. They were then ordered to cover. To a woman, the *khimār* is the same as a turban to a man."'
- Although essentially the *khimār* is a head covering, it may happen that a woman covers her face, or part of it, with her *khimār*, i.e. with her head covering. There is a real difference between this and saying that *ikhtamarn* means they covered their faces. This latter statement suggests that the essential meaning of the *khimār* is face covering, which is wrong.

★ ★ ★ ★ ★ ★

People say that the books of hadith mention the following: 'A woman came to Samurah ibn Jundab and told him that her husband did not have sex with her. He asked the man but he denied what she said. Samurah wrote to Muʿāwiyah consulting him. Muʿāwiyah wrote back: "Marry him to a woman with a fair share of beauty and religion, [paying for the marriage] from the treasury." Samurah did that... The woman came wearing a *qināʿ*.' This shows that women during the Prophet's companions time used to cover their faces.

In answer we say firstly that there is no denial that some Arabian women used to cover their faces before and after the advent of Islam. What is being cited of the practice of some women is no more than examples of what some women did. It does not amount to providing evidence in support of a particular view. The point in question is not whether it was done or not, but whether it is a duty or a recommended practice, or neither of these two.

Secondly, when we look at the meaning of the word *qinā'* in Arabic dictionaries, we realise that it does not mean covering one's face. On the contrary, *Lisān al-'Arab* makes clear that it refers to 'the garment a woman uses to cover her head and charms. They may refer to grey hair as a *qinā'* because it grows on the head, which is where a *qinā'* is worn. A *muqanna'* [i.e. a person wearing a *qinā'*] is one who is covering his head.'

- In al-Bukhari's *Ṣaḥīḥ*: Chapter: Wearing a *qinā'*. Ibn 'Abbās said: 'The Prophet came out wearing a turban that had darkened in colour.' A hadith entered in this chapter is narrated by 'Ā'ishah who says: '... As we were seated in our home around midday, someone said to Abu Bakr: "Here is God's Messenger coming, wearing a *qinā'* at a time when he used not to come to us."' In *Fatḥ al-Bārī*, [which is Ibn Ḥajar's voluminous commentary on al-Bukhari's *Ṣaḥīḥ*]: '... Al-Ismā'īlī said: "What he mentioned of turban does not involve wearing a *qinā'*, which means covering one's head"... "wearing a *qinā'* means covering his head."'

The author adds here several quotations from books of commentary on the Qur'an and the hadith, all of which explain the *qinā'* as head covering. He finally says:

It is true that Ibn Ḥajar says elsewhere that wearing a *qinā'* means 'covering the head and most of the face with a garment or some other thing'. However, we should understand this as happening on occasions, not all the time. Otherwise, we will be contradicting all these texts that explain the *qinā'* as only a head cover. In other words, a *qinā'* is essentially a head covering, but at times it means also covering a small portion of one's face in addition to one's head.

CHAPTER IV

The Debate: Is Face-Covering Recommended for Women?

People cite the following hadith: Qays ibn Shammās narrated: 'A woman called Umm Khallād came to the Prophet wearing a *niqab* and asking information about her son who was killed. Some of the Prophet's Companions said to her: "Have you come to ask about your son and you are wearing a veil?" She said: "I may have the calamity of losing my son, but I shall not lose my modesty." God's Messenger said to her: "Your son shall have the reward of two martyrs." She asked: "Why is it so, Messenger of God?" He said: "Because he was killed by people who follow earlier revelations."' (Related by Abu Dāwūd) They argue that this is a clear text in praise of the *niqab* as the woman considered it an aspect of modesty and the Prophet approved.

In answer we say:

- This hadith has a chain of transmission which lacks authenticity, and as such it cannot be cited as evidence. This is what is stated about it by Shaykh Nāṣir al-Dīn al-Albānī in his book *Ḥijāb al-Mar'ah al-Muslimah*. He confirms this with quotations from al-Bukhari and Abu Ḥātim al-Rāzī.
- If, for argument's sake, we consider it authentic, it does not clearly state that the *niqab*, or veil, is preferable. The Prophet's Companions said to her: 'Have you come to ask about your son and you are wearing a veil?' This question signifies disapproval of her action, or at least amazement at it. It was well known among the Arabs, before and after Islam, that a woman who habitually wears a *niqab* takes it off at times of calamity.
- That she considered wearing the *niqab* an aspect of modesty was her own view. The Prophet approved of her personal view, which means that her action was permissible as was her view that it was an aspect of modesty. Moreover, the Prophet did not question the propriety of his Companions' disapproval. In other words, he approved the woman's action and his Companions' objection to it.
- Had the *niqab* been recommended, the Prophet's Companions would not have objected to it. Indeed, they would not have disapproved of it if it was appropriate at a time of calamity. Clothes are worn every day by all people, and what is appropriate or preferable is well-known to all. Had the *niqab* been recommended, she would have said: 'Do you object to me doing what is best?' Or, 'How come you wonder at the better and more fitting action?'

She mentions modesty and this is merely an expression of her own feeling if she discards her familiar type of dress. Her modesty in this case is similar to that of a man who meets people without his turban when he normally wears it. Had wearing it been recommended, the

Prophet would have informed his Companions of their mistake and would have disapproved of their objection to the woman's behaviour when it was the better and preferable option.

★ ★ ★ ★ ★ ★

People say that covering the woman's face is recommended because it helps to check the moral corruption that has swept many contemporary Muslim societies where most women leave their faces uncovered.

Our answer makes two points. The first is that we acknowledge that moral corruption has swept many contemporary Muslim societies, but to think that uncovering the woman's face is the reason, or one of the reasons, for this trend is untrue. These societies differ from the more conservative ones by the fact that women there reveal far more than their faces, including their heads, necks, a portion of their chests, arms and chins. This, rather than the mere face-uncovering, is a basic factor in the spread of moral corruption. There are many other factors, including the Western cultural invasion that encourages many deviant forms. We may stress here the added importance of what is carried by the media, in its different forms. Other factors include weakness of the religious sense due to wrong upbringing, the weakness of family control and public complacency at the spread of sinful behaviour.

The problem is further aggravated by the economic and social conditions that lead to the delay of young people's marriage for many years. This often helps the spread of immorality.

It is fair to attribute the spread of moral corruption to all these factors, and not limit it to merely the uncovering of the woman's face.

Secondly, we certainly lack data and field studies about Muslim communities where women cover their faces and others where they do not. However, Muslim societies have had a long experience, over many centuries, and its effects are well known. This helps us to arrive at correct conclusions which are not influenced by personal views or common delusions. In rural societies in Egypt and many other Muslim countries women do not cover their faces, while in urban society women used to cover their faces until the early twentieth century. Yet the general religious atmosphere is largely similar in both types of society. The question is: was moral corruption widespread in rural society because of the uncovering of women's faces? In contrast, did urban society adhere better to moral values because its women covered their faces? I do not think we can make any such assumption. Indeed, the opposite is true. Rural society was always more serious and steady than urban society. Perhaps if we carry proper studies giving us accurate data we may discover that uncovering women's faces, rather than covering them, helps to maintain the general morality of contemporary Muslim society, despite the corruption that affects some of its aspects.

For a fuller discussion, reference may be made to Chapter 4 of Volume 4.

★ ★ ★ ★ ★ ★

People say: If there is no clear evidence to recommend covering women's faces, we may consider it an aspect of piety, and piety is commendable.

Our answer makes the following points:

- There is a difference between piety as personal conduct and piety in issuing rulings. In personal conduct piety may mean avoiding something permissible because of an occasional element of suspicion. Piety in issuing rulings means very careful study of God's legislation. It is imperative that we must not give a ruling of permissibility to something that is reprehensible. Likewise we cannot give a ruling which pronounces something as reprehensible when it is in fact permissible. Nor is it appropriate to give a ruling of recommendation if the matter in question is merely permissible. In God's law, there is no difference between making what is forbidden lawful and forbidding what is lawful. Likewise, there is no difference between legalising what is reprehensible and discouraging what is permissible. Finally, there is no difference between forbidding what is permissible and making it a duty or recommended. All such actions encroach on God's authority to legislate.

- Islamic law works on the principle of making things easier for people and removing their hardship. It is not based on pious avoidance. Yet piety is a virtue that people are encouraged to have. However, as al-Shawkānī says: 'Abandoning what is permissible is not piety.'
- In general, neither the uncovering of the woman's face nor men looking at women's faces casts any doubt about the permissibility of it remaining uncovered. This is something that applies to all societies in different degrees. We have mentioned several incidents during the Prophet's lifetime when men looked at women's faces, but this did not make the Prophet recommend women to cover their faces as an act of piety.

★ ★ ★ ★ ★ ★

People say that the *niqab* was, in the past, a common healthy practice and a mark of women who were highly virtuous. This shows that it is a recommended practice because it helps the woman maintain her modesty and chastity.

In reply we say that the *niqab* was merely a type of clothing some women chose in pre-Islamic days, and people accepted it. Perhaps they considered it distinctive of a highly moral lady or adding to a woman's proper appearance. It was not a common healthy practice among all the Arabs who were the first to be addressed by the Islamic message. Had it been so, particularly for ladies of high morality, the Prophet's home would have been the first to implement it, right from the early days of Islam until the revelation of the *ḥijāb* verse. This would have been good evidence confirming that wearing a *niqab* was recommended. However, it is certain, on the basis of authentic and clear texts, that the Prophet's wives did not wear the *niqab*, but continued to uncover their faces until the *ḥijāb* was made obligatory on them.[18] This confirms that the *niqab* was merely a type of dress some women used. Since the Prophet's wives uncovered their faces before the *ḥijāb* was made obligatory on them, other Muslim women did the same. Indeed, Muslim women generally remained the same after the *ḥijāb* applied to the Prophet's wives. In other words, most of them did not cover their faces. So what is new, then, warranting a change in the ruling concerning the *niqab*, where it goes from permissible to recommended? The many texts we have cited confirm that nothing changed in the case of Muslim women generally after the *ḥijāb* was made obligatory for the Prophet's wives only.

What preserves a woman's modesty and chastity is, in the first place, her fear of God, then implementing the proper manners of meeting between men and women, which do not include covering women's faces. Had such covering been the only thing that would preserve a woman's modesty and chastity, God would have made it obligatory or strongly recommended it to all Muslim women.

★ ★ ★ ★ ★ ★

18. Chapter 3, Volume 4 discusses that the Prophet's wives did not cover their faces before the *ḥijāb* verse made it obligatory on them and that it did not apply to other Muslim women after its revelation. – Author's note.

People say that the *niqab* is permissible and it has been practised and encouraged in many Muslim countries for centuries.

We say in answer that there is no disagreement about the permissibility of the *niqab*, or that it has been practised in some Muslim countries. The disagreement is about its being encouraged. If it means that it was encouraged by tradition, we do not disagree. Tradition differs from one place to another. Covering women's faces may earn praise in one country or province while another country praises keeping the woman's face uncovered. If, on the other hand, it is meant that it is encouraged from the Islamic point of view, i.e. it is ruled as recommended in Islam, this requires clear evidence. We have not been able to find such evidence so far. If clear evidence is cited, we bow to it. Islam is God's law and we worship Him by following His law and guidance, with neither addition nor omission.

★ ★ ★ ★ ★ ★

Such are the arguments presented by people who say that covering the woman's face is recommended, and our answers. We have a few words more to say to them:

First, recommendation and encouragement come from God, the Legislator. Why, then, do we not have a clear text urging covering the woman's face, despite its being a matter of concern to all women? Indeed it is also of concern to all men, because every man has female companions: a wife, a mother, a sister or a daughter.

Secondly, it is important to remember that the permissibility of uncovering the woman's face is not only due to the burden face covering represents. Had it been so, it would have been said that such a burden should be tolerated for the sake of removing temptation. After all, the burden is light and the benefit is great. The fact is that uncovering the woman's face serves several interests, in addition to removing the burden and hardship a woman bears when she covers her face. We mentioned these interests in our discussion of the evidence supporting the permissibility of uncovering women's faces. Moreover, face covering is attended by several risks, in addition to its being burdensome. We discussed both these interests and risks in Chapter 4, Volume 4.

Thirdly, although we are in favour of keeping the woman's face uncovered, due to the several interests it serves, and we reject, on the basis of evidence, the argument that face covering is recommended in all situations, we do not ignore that such cover may be recommended for some individuals in particular situations. However, this is subject to the judgement of the individual; it cannot be the basis of a general ruling. Examples of such special situations include the scenario of a woman being harassed by fixed lusty looks, and a scenario when she realises that the matter is not confined to casual looks; it may lead to some serious risks.

Fourthly, there is no way to deal with the temptation associated with women except through the method stated by God, the Legislator. It begins with strengthening faith in people's hearts, enhancing their God-fearing sense and their adherence to His rulings, and training them on these. Lowering their gaze is one such ruling. When it is implemented it reflects firm belief and a strong sense of God fearingness. When it is disregarded, it reflects unfirm belief and a weak sense of God-fearingness. Therefore, we say that if this practice is neglected, the only remedy is to revive God's method through the consolidation of faith, enhancement of the sense of God-fearingness, abiding by Islamic rulings and training in all these. To seek an alternative to this very effective method, opting for a superficial action, namely, covering women's faces, and then to imagine that we have dealt with the problem is the wrong way. It simply provides a useless treatment based on an erroneous assumption. It may provide a superficial treatment of the problem but it certainly does not touch its roots. All that it achieves is to prevent looking at women in public, but in private it does nothing: the weak man will continue to cast stealthy looks and the weak woman will continue to uncover when she thinks that nobody is watching.

One of the proofs of the invalidity of such thinking is the fact that God has made lowering the gaze a value that applies to men and women alike. Covering the woman's face only deals with the surface of the problem in respect of the man only and in public. The woman receives no help despite the moral deterioration of people and the weakness of men. She can still look through her face covering. What is worse is that this covering allows the weak woman to cast fixed looks as she remains unnoticed by those around.

Fifthly, we say to those who insist that covering the woman's face is recommended: do not think that your view has been upheld for a long time and that its negation is a new development influenced by the practices of Western society. *Qadi* 'Iyāḍ (died 544 AH, 1150 CE) said: 'The Prophet's wives alone were told to cover their faces and hands as a duty, but scholars have different views on whether it is recommended for other women.'

Final Comments on the Debate

We need to pause long in order to fully understand the meaning of the *ḥijāb* which was made obligatory on the Prophet's wives alone, and not to any other believing women. It is one type of *ḥijāb* and it is given in a very clear statement that does not allow different interpretation. It is a screen that makes them personally unseen: 'When you ask the Prophet's wives for something, do so from behind a screen.' (33: 53) Their voices were not suppressed, nor were men's voices suppressed. This means that they continued to deal with men, but from behind a screen. They continued to move about, and they accompanied the Prophet on his travels. They remained active, without restriction, whether their activity was religious, social or political. They did not stop taking interest in, and interacting with the world around them. We provided evidence confirming all these points in Chapter 3, Volume 2.

These are not words we make casually. We have evidence confirming every word we have stated.

In the long age of backwardness Muslims have gone through, they made this *ḥijāb* which was obligatory for the Prophet's wives, but not for their own women, thick layers of covering which they placed on top of each other. Had they covered the woman's face with a *niqab* which left the eyes uncovered, we would have said that this was the custom of some Arabian women in pre-Islamic days and the Prophet approved of it. They covered the Muslim woman's face with something that hid all her face, in a strange and ugly way.

Having covered the woman's face, why did they also prevent her speech, despite its being permissible as indicated by God's words in His address to the Prophet's wives: 'Speak in an appropriate manner.' (33: 32)

Having covered the woman's face, why did they stop her going to the mosque despite the Prophet's clear injunction: 'Do not prevent women servants of God from attending God's mosques,' and despite the fact that the Prophet's female Companions joined obligatory, *tarāwīḥ*, eclipse and funeral prayers in the Prophet's mosque?

Having covered the woman's face, why did they stop her attending the Eid Prayer, although the hadith says: 'The Prophet commanded us to bring out the young women and those secluded at home... so that they witness the goodness and share in the Muslims' supplication.'

Having covered the woman's face, why did they stop her attending lectures and seminars, when the hadith says: 'A woman came to the Prophet and said: "Messenger of God, the men have monopolized your teachings. Allocate a day for us when we come and you teach us as God has taught you." He said: "Assemble on such-and-such day at such place."'

Having covered the woman's face, why did they stop her from fulfilling the task of enjoining what is right and forbidding what is wrong. Yet Umm al-Dardā', a Companion of the Prophet, said to Caliph 'Abd al-Malik ibn Marwān: 'You cursed your servant when God's Messenger says: "Those who curse shall not be intercessors or witnesses on the Day of Judgement."'

Having covered the woman's face, why did they prevent her from working to earn her living when necessary, despite the fact that the Prophet said to a woman who was still in her waiting period: 'Yes, you may pick up your fruit. You may give some to charity or do some kindly deed.'

Having covered the woman's face, why did they prevent her from joining in jihad, attending to the wounded and giving water to the thirsty, and fighting when necessary. Yet some of the female Companions of the Prophet joined several military expeditions.

Having covered the woman's face, why did they stop her participation in social and political activity, despite the confirmation that Umm Sharīk's home was open to all guests, some women attended the Anṣar's pledge to the Prophet at 'Aqabah, many women pledged their allegiance to the Prophet after the Hijrah and despite the hadith in which the Prophet says: 'We extend protection to those you have protected, Umm Hāni'.'

Having covered the woman's face so that it could not be seen by anyone, why did they also prevent her being seen by the one who is proposing to marry her, while the Prophet said to the one making a proposal: '... Go and look at her.'

Having covered the woman's face, why did they also prevent describing her appearance, as if it is also *'awrah* and should be covered lest men are tempted when it is mentioned. Yet hadiths include such description: 'a woman with dark red cheeks', a 'white woman', 'a pretty woman from Khath'am'. And 'Diḥyah had a pretty maid in his share of war gains.'

Having covered the woman's face, why did they prevent mentioning her news, as if these are *'awrah* like her face and must be covered. This despite the fact that the Qur'an and the hadiths include much of what relates to women. The Qur'an mentions what the wife of the Egyptian chief and her friends did. The hadiths include much of the news of the Prophet's wives and the news of a good number of the Prophet's female Companions, such as how Umm Sulaym wore makeup and made herself available to her husband on the day their son died, how Asmā' bint Abu Bakr managed matters so that she would not stir her husband's jealousy and how Asmā' bint 'Umays bravely countered 'Umar ibn al-Khaṭṭāb's remarks.

Having covered the woman's face, why did they stop mentioning her name, as if its mere mention would give the smell of sex! Yet God mentions in the Qur'an Maryam bint 'Imran, and the Prophet says: "Ā'ishah entered,' 'I said to Ḥafṣah,' and 'This is Ṣafiyyah.'

★ ★ ★ ★ ★ ★

Therefore, we need to establish 'the point of contention' as scholars of Fiqh say. In other words, we need to clarify the subject matter of this long dispute. The dispute is not about covering the woman's face or not, but is rather a much bigger one. It is about keeping this human being, the woman, secluded, depriving her of gaining experience, awareness and knowledge and keeping her 'under house arrest', as it were. It is about depriving society of whatever good the woman can give in addition to her essential task of looking after her family home and being a good wife. The point of contention is the emancipation of the Muslim woman so that she can live her life fully and interact with a serious and goodly life. Keeping her face uncovered is merely a factor that helps in the achievement of this goal.

Fine Words Addressed to All Participants in the Debate

We now conclude this debate with those who take their stand against leaving the woman's face uncovered with these remarks by an eminent scholar. He said:

> We have discussed this question at length because people need to know the ruling on this serious social issue. Many of those who support the discarding of cover have tackled this question without sufficient research and exploration. Yet it is the duty of every fair and honest writer to learn before he speaks, and to look at the evidence on both sides like an arbiter listening to two disputants. He should consider in fairness and rule on the basis of knowledge, giving no preference to either side unless it has a clear basis. He should look at the evidence from all sides. If he shares one of the two views in conflict, this should not lead him to excess in confirming its argument and evidence, ignoring or discarding the evidence of the opposite view. Hence, scholars said that a scholar must look at the evidence before forming an opinion, so that his opinion should be based on evidence, not leading it. A person who formulates his view before looking at the evidence may resort to rejecting texts that are contrary to his view, or to twisting them if he cannot reject them. We, as others, have seen the negative consequences of looking for evidence in support of an already formulated view. This leads a person to grade as authentic hadiths that are seriously lacking in authenticity, or to attach to authentic texts significance that is alien to them, only to confirm his own view and find supporting arguments for it.

These are valuable words of which I remind myself and my brethren who take the opposite view to mine. I hope these words will benefit us all. A person is weak on his own, strong when having his brethren's support. Likewise, his reasoning is weak on its own, but it is strengthened with the reasoning of his brethren. Debate helps to bring minds together in order to ascertain the truth. No matter how hard the debate is, we must continue to work together and cooperate so that we get to the truth together, or at least get closer to the truth.

We all seek God's guidance, as He alone guides along the right way.